Horsemanship Handbook

SUSAN J. STUSKA, ED. D   EIGHTH EDITION

HOBAR

Notice to the Reader
The information and material in this manual are accurate and true to the best of
our knowledge. All recommendations are made without guarantee on the part of
the author or Hobar Publications. The author and publisher disclaim any liability in
connection with the use of information contained in this book or the application of
such information. For additional information, please contact Hobar Publications.

The publisher advises the reader of this book to consult and work with an
experienced horseperson to reinforce the material described within this book. The
reader is expressly warned to consider and adopt all safety precautions regarding
horses and to avoid all potential hazards. By following the instructions contained
herein, the reader willingly assumes all risks in connection with such instructions.

Hobar Publications
3943 Meadowbrook Road
Minneapolis, MN 55426-4505
A DIVISION OF FINNEY COMPANY

Phone: (952) 938-9330 or (800) 846-7027
Fax: (952) 938-7353
Website: www.finney-hobar.com

TABLE OF CONTENTS & LIST OF ILLUSTRATIONS

Section 5: Area Work

PREFACE

The *Horsemanship Handbook* is designed to provide, in one place, the theory, philosophy, and factual information that is so important to the student during the early stages of horseback riding. It is designed to supplement the information provided by riding instructors and allow the instructors to concentrate on teaching the skills while the text covers the "book knowledge." This text provides study materials for students and a common body of knowledge that can be tested by the instructor as appropriate. It also emphasizes and reminds the student of the concepts covered in riding classes. Riders working alone may also use this text to their advantage. Riding-instructors-in-training will find the explanations useful while building their repertoire of teaching techniques.

Specifics of hunt-, stock-, and saddle-seat disciplines are included. Riders of these disciplines, as well as balance-seat riders and those working toward dressage, will benefit; many of the basics are shared among these riding styles.

It is the intent of this text to facilitate an understanding of and communication with the horse and to stress safety. It is hoped that the information here will benefit all riding students who strive to master the art and science of horsemanship.

Sue Stuska
Smyrna, North Carolina
July 2003

SINCERE APPRECIATION

For the illustrations to:

    Peggy Judy, Caduceus Farm, Ltd., for the majority of the illustrations that are new for this edition;

    USA Equestrian for the curb chains;

    Sterling Publishing Company, Inc., and artist Jeanne Mellin for the cut-back saddle and the show bridle;

    Robyn McGovern for the parts of the stock saddle.

To the Appaloosa Horse Club for the information on Appaloosa coat patterns.

To Alan E. Krysan, President, Finney Company, for the impetus in creating this eighth edition.

To Beatrice Wellborn and the Hobar staff for their patient proofreading (any further mistakes are mine alone).

To the most enthusiastic of my riding students, whose desire to get the most out of every riding session prompted the writing and updating of the *Horsemanship Handbook*.

To my parents; they've been my supporters since my childhood when they watched my first riding lessons and then reviewed what I'd learned afterwards.

And to my husband, Dr. Neil Murphy, who, as an educator, understands and supports my writing and teaching.

SAFETY RULES AND PRECAUTIONS

Safety around horses involves knowledge of their possible reactions to any given stimulus, an effort to anticipate these reactions, and an attempt to stay out of harm's way while still being in control of the situation. Working with horses involves risk, but safety education and preventative practices do minimize the risk. Most accidents are caused by the rider failing to think about safety. With practice, safe procedures will become second nature. Constant attention to the situation will best prevent accidents.

This chapter covers the basic and important safety measures. Further references to safe practices may be found in other chapters; please refer to these, as well. Barns and riding facilities will also have their own written or unwritten safely rules and regulations.

Working around the Horse

1. Stay in the safety zone—close to the shoulder, barrel, or hip—whenever possible. Avoid staying in front of or behind the horse, and when you are there, constantly monitor the horse's ears and other body language. Keep your feet clear of the horse's feet, and keep your head away from its head and legs.

2. Move around the horse's hindquarters either by keeping your hand firmly on its croup and staying close or by walking a horse's length away.

3. Never kneel or sit on the ground anywhere near a horse. Do not put your hands down on the ground where they might get stepped on.

4. Never place yourself between a horse and an object to which the animal is tied. Do not go under the rope of a tied horse. If the animal is startled, pulls back and feels the restraint, and then moves forward, the horse might hurt you.

5. Select horses that match your capabilities as a horse person and rider. In general, the less experienced the rider/handler, the more experienced and predictable the horse should be. Horse suitability for the type of riding and use (trail riding, showing, etc.) must also be considered. Instructors and trainers need to make appropriate selections in lesson, leasing, and sales situations.

6. You must have the horse's respect and attention at all times in order to be safely in control. To gain respect and attention does not mean that you need to be rough or abusive, but rather that you become a student of horse psychology so you can influence the animal to pay attention and recognize you as worthy of respect.

Holding the Horse

You will soon have the opportunity to hold a horse for someone else; perhaps your instructor is checking the wound you found while grooming, or you have been asked to hold a horse for shoeing. Holding a horse while someone else works on it is a situation of responsibility, because you have the opportunity to keep that person from harm. Inattention on your part can get someone hurt. There is room for personal preference, but certain safe practices are standard. Your instructor or the vet or farrier will show you the details when you ask for their preferences for how you hold the horse. For this discussion, we will generalize and call this person the worker.

1. Generally hold the halter rope 6 to 12 inches from the halter. In some cases, it is appropriate to hold the halter itself, but holding the halter often does not give you any additional control and may keep you from letting go before getting jerked around. Regardless, rely on the horse's training, and give the animal some slack in the lead rope; holding the horse tightly will mostly just make the animal uncomfortable with being so closely restrained. If you have any question about how to maneuver the horse, take a few minutes to find out before the work begins.

2. Face the worker and horse by holding the rope beneath the halter in your hand nearest the horse (left if on the left side of the horse) and the end of the rope looped across your other hand.

3. Always pay attention to the person working on the horse and to what the individual is doing. (Holding the horse is not necessarily going to let you watch the process, so you may need a third person if you are supposed to be concentrating on watching the process instead of controlling the horse.) If the situation is potentially painful (medicating a wound, for example), you will need to be prepared for the horse to move away during the process. If the worker has switched from front to hind legs, your position should change, too.

4. Always pay attention to the horse. Try to anticipate what the animal might do, which way it might move, and how comfortable or potentially uncomfortable the horse might be (perhaps the flies are bothersome that day).

5. Your job is to keep the horse's attention on you in case you need to move the animal and possibly to distract the horse from what is being done to it. In some situations, it is best if the animal stays alert to both you and the worker so the horse is not surprised by any action on the part of the worker.

6. When the front of the horse is the focus (neck, chest, shoulder, foreleg, saddle, etc.), you should be far enough to the front and side to not be in danger yourself from the horse or to be in the way of the worker but to still be in control. Generally, stay on the same side as the worker, and be ready to tip the horse's nose slightly toward you and move the horse's shoulder away from you both. Alternately, stand on the opposite side of the horse from the worker, and be ready to move the forehand a step toward you (away from the worker). Do not let the horse pivot or turn so far toward you that its hindquarters endanger the worker.

7. When the horse's hindquarters are the focus, stay on the same side as the worker and approximately opposite the horse's shoulder. Here you have the influence to move the horse's hindquarters away from the worker (by bringing its head toward you) and thus prevent injury from being stepped on or kicked. The horse should not be allowed to walk forward, because this movement puts the worker in the potential kick zone.

Tying

1. Learn simple means of restraint, and use the means to hold the horse safely. For example, cross tying involves tying the horse with two ropes, one from each side of its halter, to strong posts or substantial walls on either side. This procedure keeps the horse stationary in an open area. Other common means of restraint are tying the horse with a bowline or a quick-release knot by the animal's halter rope.

   Be aware that a loose horse that seems content to stand while you work around it may decide to move at any time. If the animal does move, it may put you in a dangerous position or go running free. It is always safer to properly restrain a horse while you work around the animal.

   Some horses may be safely groomed while standing unrestrained in a box stall with the door almost completely closed; in other cases, this practice is risky. Check with your instructor for instructions.

2. Those who work around horses should carry a sharp pocket knife in case of emergency; it is not always possible to get to the knot or to get it loose in a hurry, and it may be necessary to cut a rope.

3. Tie the horse short enough so the animal cannot get its head down and its foot over the rope. Being tangled in the rope may panic the horse. Leave the horse enough slack that the animal can move its head freely from side to side and hold it comfortably.

4. Tie the rope at or above the horse's nose level. Make certain the knot will not slip down toward the ground.

5. Never tie a horse by the bridle reins or wrap the reins around any object. If the horse pulls, the animal may break the bridle or reins and could injure its mouth.

6. Putting a halter on over the bridle and tying a horse (except for cross tying) risks a bruised or cut mouth. The horse may catch the bridle on something and then pull back.

7. The horse must be tied by a sturdy halter and rope to a solid object firmly buried in the ground. A frightened horse dragging something by its halter rope is likely to hurt itself and cause a lot of damage. A horse that repeatedly breaks free may learn to pull back hard whenever it feels pressure on its head. This handbook assumes the horse has

been successfully taught to stand tied (a process that includes the horse consistently and immediately giving to pressure on its head). Your instructor will advise you of the appropriate restraint for the horse(s) you work with.

8. Untie the halter rope before unhaltering the horse and before slipping the halter back around its neck to restrain the horse for bridling. You will not get caught if the animal throws its head or turns away, and the horse will not be caught with the halter around its neck if the animal should panic and pull back. Putting the bridle reins over the horse's neck will give you an additional handle on the animal. Keep the reins far enough off the ground so that neither you nor the horse will step on or through them.

9. Never use clippers, brushes, spray bottles, aerosol cans, etc., on the face, head, neck, chest or front legs of a horse that is tied. Untie the horse first, and stand to the side of its head.

Leading

1. Walk beside the horse when leading. If you walk out in front of the animal, particularly with a long length of lead rope between you and the horse, and the horse jumps forward, it may step on you.

2. Use both hands: the right hand holds the lead rope or reins under the horse's chin, and the left hand holds the end of the rope to keep it off the ground. Lay the excess rope in loops across your left hand (rather than coil it where you might get caught if the coils tighten). If the horse should rear or pull away, you have the added grasp of your left hand on the end of the lead to keep from losing the horse.

·3. Your horse is stronger than you, so do not try to outpull the animal. If the horse tries to move too quickly or in a different direction and does not pay attention to you, either 1) step to a position at an angle to the horse's head and hold the lead firmly until the animal gives to pressure or 2) give a quick tug or snap on the lead rope. (Check with your instructor for details of the horse's training.)

4. Never wrap lead ropes, longe lines, or reins around your hand, wrist, or body. Always keep a secure hold on the lead rope.

5. Gloves should be worn; they protect your hands from rope burns if the horse should try to pull away. Even the most docile horse may become frightened, and there is always the variable of other horses moving around in the area.

6. If the horse hangs back and refuses to lead, do not pull the animal forward. Either 1) stay in your leading position near the horse's neck and dislodge its front feet to the left or right until the horse moves, and then proceed forward, or 2) use the tail of your long lead rope to encourage the horse forward from behind. (Check with your instructor for the preferred way to handle this situation.)

7. Open doors all the way and make certain that the latches are flush with the door to prevent hang-ups and injuries. Turn and watch as your horse walks through gates and doors to prevent the animal from bumping or catching itself. Always go through narrow doorways ahead of the horse and step to the side while maintaining control as the horse follows.

8. When leading the horse into a box stall, walk all the way in, turn the horse so that the animal faces the door, and close the door before you release the horse.

9. When turning the horse loose in a field or other enclosure, walk through the gate, close it, walk into the field a short distance, and turn the horse so it faces the gate before you release the animal. This way the horse has to turn around before running off, and you will have time and space to get out of the animal's way if the horse should kick as it is turned loose.

Most facilities avoid turning horses loose with halters on because of the danger of the halter getting caught on an object (including the horse's own shoe heel). Nylon halters, designed not to break, are particularly dangerous, while leather halters may break in an emergency. Halters with breakaway sections are available.

Never gesture at or hit a horse to encourage the animal to leave you. This practice encourages dangerous behavior: breaking away before the horse is released and kicking out when it leaves.

10. Always run up English stirrups when you are not in the saddle so they stay out of the way and do not catch on anything. Watch western stirrups; they are less likely to catch on objects but still can.

Tacking Up

1. Keep tack off the ground at all times. Putting the saddle on the ground may save you a few minutes but can also cause discomfort to the horse from dirt on the pad and cost money if the tack is damaged (by being stepped on).

2. Stand beside—not in front of—the horse when bridling; keep your head clear.

3. Check reins, cheek pieces, girth, cinch, stirrup leathers, latigo, and billets for wear, cracking, or loose stitching every day. Failure of any of these parts can result in injury. Keep tack clean, and oil it as needed to prolong its life.

4. Recheck the girth/cinch after riding a few minutes, and tighten it if necessary.

Mounting and Dismounting

1. Pick an open space without projections or overhangs for mounting. Stay clear of other horses. If your horse takes a step as you swing up, the animal will not endanger you or itself.

2. Choose a mounting area with secure footing, i.e. grass, dirt, or gravel. Avoid asphalt or concrete; these surfaces can be slippery and are harder than other surfaces if you should fall.

3. From the ground, adjust the reins so that there is some slack, and then place your left hand and the reins on the horse's neck near the withers. Hold the mane so you do not risk pulling on the horse's mouth when you mount. By holding a handful of mane, you give yourself a secure hold while avoiding pulling out the mane hairs. Pulling on the mane does not hurt or bother the vast majority of horses. With four reins, leave the curb reins much looser than the snaffle reins.

4. The horse should stand still for mounting. This stillness is important for your safety. If you make the process comfortable for the horse (by not pulling its mouth, wrenching the saddle around, etc.), the animal will be more willing to stand. Your instructor will help you learn to ask the horse to stand while you mount. Although you will learn to mount from the ground, a mounting block is much easier on the horse's back. Many facilities use blocks routinely for this reason.

5. While mounted, hold the reins at all times to keep control of your horse, including times when you are adjusting English stirrups or tightening the girth. When putting on or taking off your coat, it is safest to dismount. The coat might flap and scare the horse (particularly if it is a rain slicker), or something might happen while your arms are pinned or your vision is obstructed.

6. Keep both feet in the stirrups and stay alert while adjusting English stirrups or tightening the girth to keep your balance; the horse might move suddenly. Even the most quiet horse may spook at an unaccustomed noise or movement.

7. When dismounting, keep control. Choose a safe landing spot with secure footing. While you will be expected to either slide down (taking the left foot out of the stirrup immediately after you swing your right foot over if you ride English style) or step down (touch the ground with your right foot before taking the left foot out of the stirrup if you ride western style), you should also know how to take both feet out of the stirrups and vault off (sometimes called an emergency dismount). In both slide-down and step-down dismounts, back your left foot out of the stirrup a little before you swing your right leg over, so you can remove your foot easily at the appropriate time.

   Keep both hands on the horse (usually the left hand on the mane with the reins and the right hand on the saddle) until you are safely on the ground. This way you can avoid losing your balance and falling backward. If you falter when dismounting and are holding the reins off the horse's neck, you can pull the horse toward you where the animal might step on you.

8. To keep control of the horse, bring your reins over the horse's head (if joined) or off the animal's neck (if split) as soon as you are safely on the ground, and hold them correctly. Never let the reins hang on the ground; the horse could step on them and hurt its mouth or step though them and get tangled. You do not want to step on or through the reins either. Keeping them off the ground also keeps the reins cleaner.

Group Riding

1. Follow at least two horse's lengths behind (more lengths the faster you are moving) to avoid irritating the horse in front of you. If the other horse should kick or stop suddenly, you will be able to avoid the animal.

2. Pass wide—three horse's widths—and always on the inside when in the arena. Avoid riding between a horse and a solid object if there is not a lot of space; avoid getting pinned between a horse and the arena rail.

3. When asking to pass someone who is improperly blocking the arena track, call "rail please" loud enough to be clearly heard and early enough so the individual can move safely.

4. When meeting another rider head-on in an arena, call "inside" or "outside" to let the rider know which way you will pass. When in doubt, pass left hand to left hand inside or outside of the arena.

5. Always look around before stopping or turning; avoid other riders who may be coming up behind you.

6. Horses traveling at faster gaits generally use the perimeter of the arena (called the rail). Horses that are standing or walking should be toward the center of the arena.

7. All riders in an arena should yield right of way to beginners, young children, and riders on less experienced horses.

8. Time your arena entrance or departure so as not to cause interference with others. Calling "gate" or "door" will alert other riders to your intention of coming in or going out and give them time to avoid you.

Rider Equipment

1. Smooth-soled boots with heels are required to give the necessary ankle and foot support, to protect your ankles from the stirrup leathers and your toes from being stepped on, to keep your feet from sliding too far into the stirrup, and to enable you to slip your feet out of the stirrups quickly in an emergency.

2. Wear a helmet that meets the American Society for Testing and Materials (ASTM) standards, is certified by the Safety Equipment Institute (SEI), and is fitted according to the organizations' recommendations. The harness must be fastened for maximum protection. Helmets are traditional for hunt-seat riders, are essential for jumping, and are an excellent idea for western and saddle-seat riders, too. If your helmet is involved in a fall, is dropped, or is crushed, it must be returned to the manufacturer for repair or replacement. Do not wear such headgear, even if it looks undamaged. Its protection ability may have been compromised.

3. Do not chew gum while riding to avoid the possibility of choking on it.

4. Jewelry, particularly that which dangles or projects outward, can be dangerous. It can catch on tack. It can also be distracting. Most riders wear minimal jewelry.

General Barn Procedures

1. Smoking is generally not allowed at any time in the barn because of fire danger.

2. Always return all your equipment to its proper place to avoid damage or loss. Keep tack off the ground.

3. Stay out of the stalls and enclosures of horses that you do not know or do not have permission to work with.

4. Avoid hand-feeding horses, because they may bite. Do not tease a horse by allowing the animal to nip at your hand.

5. Running, shouting, and horseplay are inappropriate in the barn.

6. When in doubt, ask.

NOTES

2

COLORS OF HORSES

Coat colors make horses easier to identify; therefore, horse enthusiasts should have a working knowledge of horse colors and patterns. Students should learn the coat colors described below and be able to identify horses by their color. There are infinite variations in color; these variations make classification helpful but also sometimes inadequate. Genetic evaluation may be necessary to determine the exact, true color. Terms and definitions for colors vary from breed to breed and discipline to discipline; consult the breed/discipline of your choice for the most specific description.

White face markings and white on the feet may occur with all of the following colors. These markings are controlled by different genes and are therefore not necessarily related to the body color.

Basic Horse Coat Colors

Bay. A bay horse has a brownish coat that can look more red brown or more yellow brown. A light bay shows more yellow, while a dark bay shows more red. The darkest is the mahogany bay, which is almost the color of blood but without the red overtone. Bays always have a black mane and tail and black points, i.e. lower legs.

Although the body color of a bay and a chestnut may be similar, the two can always be distinguished because the bay has a black mane, tail, and points; the chestnut's points are the same color as the body or possibly lighter.

Black. Black hair over the entire body is characteristic of this color of horse. Some bleaching of the coat may occur, but the underlying skin will be black. The mane, tail, and points are always black.

Brown. Often called seal brown, this color comes from a mixture of red and liver or red and black hairs. The resulting brownish look varies in shade from light to dark in different horses and sometimes in the same horse between winter and summer. At first glance, the brown horse may look black. The lower legs, especially, may be dark enough to look black. The true brown horse should have telltale reddish hairs on the flank, muzzle, and abdomen.

Chestnut. Sometimes called sorrel, this color varies from bright yellowish red to rich mahogany red. The points are the same color as the body unless the mane and tail are straw colored (termed flaxen).

Liver. Genetically different from chestnut, this color is characterized by hairs of a uniform liver-brown color. The mane, tail, and lower legs are the same liver shade.

White. The true white horse is born completely white, with pink skin and colored eyes (blue or brown). White leg markings will not show. White horses have one gene for the color white; a pair of white genes is lethal, so an embryo/foal with this pair will die.

A faded gray will have dark skin that distinguishes the animal from a white horse.

A true albino horse would have pink skin and eyes, but evidence suggests that such horses do not exist.

Variations in Basic Coat Colors

Dun. (Buckskin) The body color of a dun may range from pale yellow to a dirty canvas color or be some shade of cream, reddish orange, or gray. A wide range of terms are used to describe the color variations. Duns usually have a dark stripe running down their back from mane to tail; this stripe is called a dorsal stripe. Buckskins may or may not have a dorsal stripe. (The Buckskin registry and the Quarter Horse registry have specific breed color descriptions.) Sometimes black horizontal stripes, called zebra stripes, are found on the legs—mostly above the knee and hocks. Dun and buckskin horses have black points. Dun or buckskin is actually a dilution of the bay color.

Grullo. Pronounced "grew' yah", this type of horse is a grayish-blue mouse color. The points are black, as is the dorsal stripe. Zebra stripes may occur. This color may be due to the dilution of dark seal brown or black.

Gray. The gray horse looks gray because of a combination of black and white hairs. The proportion of dark to light hairs determines the shade, which varies from steel gray to almost white. The color may get progressively lighter with age (called graying). The skin will always be, and the eyes are usually, dark. Dark circles, called dapples, may occur.

When small dots of black and brown are found on an otherwise white body, the color is called flea-bitten gray.

Palomino. This golden body color may range from light yellow to bright copper. The mane and tail are white. Black points are never seen. Palomino is a genetic dilution of chestnut. Because of the genes involved, breeding two palominos will usually not result in a palomino foal. Palomino is considered a color breed; palominos may be registered in the Palomino breed association.

Paint and pinto. A paint is a two- or three-colored horse that has a coat with large irregular patches of each color. A great deal of white above the knees and hocks is often an indicator of this coat color. The horse's body type must meet Quarter Horse breed specifications to be considered a paint. Pinto horses have similar coat color characteristics but no body-type restrictions (if it is a pony or a Saddlebred, for example, it is called pinto). There are both paint and pinto breed registries in which acceptable horses are recorded; pintos and paints are examples of color breeds.

Roan. A roan horse is any horse that has a coat with white hair intermingled with one or more base colors. Many roans do not change color (lighten) with age. Whether a horse is light roan or dark roan depends on the proportions of white to colored hairs. Most roans are combinations of bay, chestnut, or black with white hairs intermingled. They are known in order as red, strawberry, or blue roan. The roan color is generally not uniform, and some patches on the body will be darker than others. Most roans have a solid-colored head and points, which appear darker than the body color due to the lack of white hair. Mating two roan horses will probably decrease the foal crop, because the likelihood of getting a pair of roan genes will increase; a pair of roan genes is lethal for the embryo.

Appaloosa Coat Patterns

The Appaloosa Horse Club recognizes thirteen base coat colors, which are similar to the above. (There is some variation among the various breed registries on the color terms and descriptions of the coat colors.) In addition, the Appaloosa registry describes seven coat patterns. All horses will not be easily classified; there are many variations on the patterns, and combinations of patterns are common.

Blanket. Refers to a solid white area, which is normally over but not limited to the hip area of a darker-colored horse.

Spots. Refers to a horse with white or dark spots over some or all of its body.

Blanket with spots. Refers to a horse with a white area normally over but not limited to the hips, with dark spots located within the white. The spots are usually the same color as the base color of the horse (chestnut spots on a chestnut horse, for example). However, a horse may also have more than one color of spots.

Roan. Refers to an Appaloosa roan pattern (a mixture of white and dark hairs) and may have a lighter area on the forehead, jaw, and frontal bones of the face, and/or over the back, loin, and hips. Darker areas may appear on the frontal bones of the face, as well, and also on the legs or stifles, above the eyes, on the points of the hip, and behind the elbows.

Roan blanket. Refers to a horse that has a mixture of white and dark hairs over a portion of the body, normally over but not limited to the hip area.

Roan blanket with spots. Refers to a mixture of white and dark hairs over a portion of the body with white and/or dark spots within the roan area.

Solid. Refers to a horse that has a base color such as a chestnut, bay, etc., but has no contrasting color in the form of an Appaloosa coat pattern.

To make the Appaloosa description more specific, the portions of the body covered by the color pattern may also be indicated. In order of increasing body coverage, these are:

1. Hips.
2. Loin and hips.
3. Back and hips (markings extend over a portion of the back up to the withers).
4. Body and hips (markings extend from the hips, inclusive of a portion of the shoulders and/or neck, but do not cover the entire horse).
5. Entire body (markings cover the hips, loin, back, upper legs, shoulders, neck, and head).

Star

Stripe

Snip

Bald

Blaze

Star, Stripe, and Snip

Star and Stripe

2.1 White Face Markings

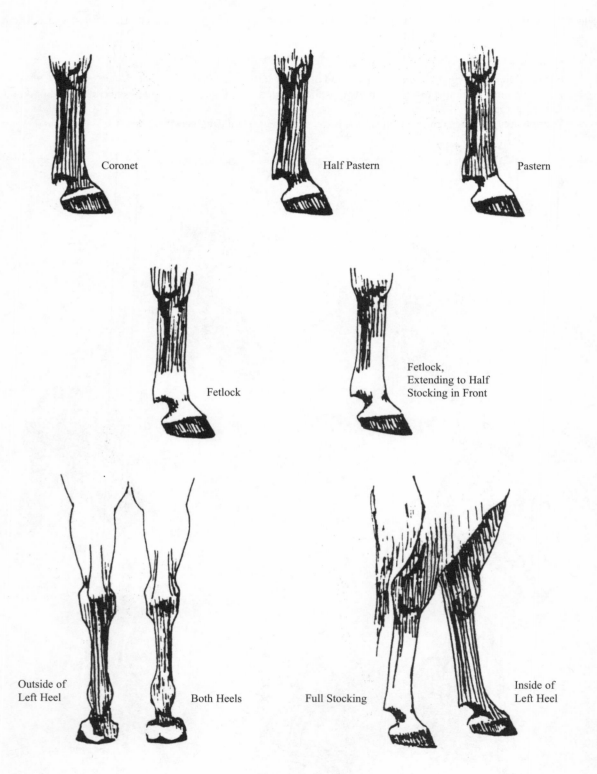

Coronet

Half Pastern

Pastern

Fetlock

Fetlock,
Extending to Half
Stocking in Front

Outside of
Left Heel

Both Heels

Full Stocking

Inside of
Left Heel

2.2 White Leg Markings

10

Horse Colors Worksheet

The horses you ride are good examples of many of the possible coat colors and patterns. Use this page to record the colors of the horses you ride. Continue until you are familiar with all of the basic coat colors and variations.

HORSE	COLOR	PATTERN & AREA	WHITE FACE MARKINGS	WHITE LEG MARKINGS

NOTES

GAITS OF THE HORSE

The gaits of horses are a fascinating study; understanding of them is important for riders. The gaits will be discussed in this order: four-beat gaits of even meter (like walk); two-beat gaits (trot, jog, and pace); three- and four-beat bounding gaits (canter, lope, hand gallop, and gallop). There are variations in the terms and definitions of these gaits between enthusiasts of different breeds and in different parts of the country.

Four-Beat Gaits of Even Meter

Walk. The walk is a four-beat gait. Each hoof moves independently; it is raised and lowered to hit the ground alone. On hard ground, you will hear four distinct, evenly spaced footfalls. There is no period of suspension (when all four feet are off the ground) in the walk, unlike the trot, pace, canter, etc. The sequence of footfalls is shown in diagram 3.1 below. Arbitrarily starting with the left hind, the sequence is:

3.1 Sequence of Footfalls in Walk

The singlefoot, a type of running walk, is a slow four-beat gait that is popular in pleasure-riding horses, because it is so smooth for the rider. Its name comes from the fact that each hoof is raised and placed on the ground separately, producing four distinct beats. No two legs move together. There are variations in this gait that are recognized in horses of various breeds; all of these four-beat gaits, executed correctly, are smooth and comfortable to ride. Missouri Foxtrotters fox trot, Tennessee Walking horses running walk, American Saddlebreds slow gait, and Paso Finos paso corto. American Saddlebreds and Paso Finos also have faster four-beat gaits. The Saddlebreds' rack can be very fast, and the Pasos emphasize rapid cadence in the paso largo.

Two-Beat Gaits

Trot. The trot is a two-beat gait. Diagonal pairs of legs move the same; one diagonal pair of hooves hits the ground together, followed by the other diagonal pair. This coordination is shown in diagram 3.2 below by the lines connecting the diagonal hooves. Watching a horse move from the side, you may be able to see the diagonal cannons moving together (roughly parallel). As the horse springs from one diagonal to the other, there is a brief period of suspension, during which all four hooves are off the ground. A stride, which is the distance from one hoof print to the next print of the same hoof, includes two brief periods of suspension if the horse is trotting. The footfalls are diagrammed below.

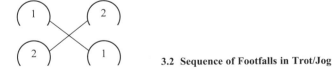

3.2 Sequence of Footfalls in Trot/Jog

Jog. The jog is a western version of the trot. It is also a two-beat diagonal gait (diagrammed the same as the trot). However, it is slower, more collected, and lacks the moments of suspension of the trot.

Pace. A horse that moves both legs on the same side forward and back at the same time is pacing. The pace is not popular in riding horses, but is often seen in racing Standard-bred horses. It is a lateral gait, and you can see the lateral legs moving roughly parallel to each other.

13

Three- and Four-Beat Bounding Gaits

Canter. This gait is a three-beat bounding gait. One hind leg begins each stride as its hoof hits the ground. The second beat is made by the diagonal pair touching down together. As the horse continues to roll forward, the remaining front leg reaches out and the hoof touches down. All four legs contribute their power to propel the horse off the ground in a low leap that is the period of suspension at canter.

Lope. This gait is the slower western version of canter. It is also a bounding three-beat gait, diagrammed the same as canter. However, it is slower, more collected, and lacks the moment of suspension of canter.

Watching a horse canter or lope, you will see that one side of the animal's body and the legs on that side reach forward more, and those hooves touch the ground farther forward in each stride than the legs on the other side. The horse is best balanced on turns if its inside legs reach more forward, or lead. Therefore, you hear of the inside (balanced) or outside (less balanced) lead. If the right legs lead, the horse is on the right lead; the left legs lead in left lead. The sequence of footfalls in both leads is shown in diagram 3.3 below.

3.3 Sequence of Footfalls in Left- and Right-Lead Canter/Lope

When cantering free around the pasture, the horse balances itself on its own by choosing the lead that is most comfortable. When you ride, you know ahead of time which way you will be turning, so you cue the horse for the appropriate lead. The signal to the horse, telling it to canter, also tells the horse which lead to take.

If the horse incorrectly takes the outside lead, it is called the wrong lead. When the rider purposely cues for the outside lead, as in a test at a horse show, for example, the horse is in counter canter.

If you want to change the horse's lead for any reason (the horse may be on the incorrect lead by accident, or you may be changing direction) the easiest thing to do is bring the horse back to trot, walk, or halt and cue for the opposite lead. This procedure is called a simple change of lead. The horse can also change its lead as the animal canters. The horse changes its body position and leg order during a period of suspension. This change is called a flying change of lead and is an advanced movement.

Sometimes the horse becomes unbalanced and does not lead with the same front leg as hind leg. The animal may be on the correct lead behind and the incorrect lead in front, or the opposite. Diagram 3.4 below shows both possibilities. This disunited canter (or lope) feels rough to the rider.

3.4 Sequence of Footfalls in Cross Canter/Lope

When you feel that the horse is unbalanced in this way, you need to correct the animal. You may bring the horse to trot or walk and start the canter/lope again, or you may signal the horse to change the incorrect legs as it canters by making half a flying change of lead.

When the horse's hindquarters are not sufficiently engaged (when they do not work hard enough to carry a sufficient portion of the animal's weight), a slow four-beat canter (or lope) occurs. The gait may feel rough, because the diagonal pair of legs hits separately, causing an additional (fourth) bump to the rider. Also, you may be able to feel the zig-zag direction of the footfalls instead of the smooth movement toward the leading foreleg.

3.5 Sequence of Footfalls in Left- and Right-Lead Four-Beat Canter/Lope

Gallop. The gallop is a fast, four-beat gait. Its sequence of footfalls is like the canter except that the horse's body, legs, and stride are stretched out so long that the diagonal pair is broken into two distinct footfalls. A lengthy period of suspension follows the four beats of the stride. The rider feels a series of leaps as the horse seems to fly over the ground. The true four-beat racing gallop is rarely seen in pleasure-riding horses, but a fast canter is also called a gallop.

3.6 Sequence of Footfalls in Left- and Right-Lead Gallop

A hand gallop is sometimes asked of show horses in hunter classes; this gallop is actually a fast, controlled three-beat canter.

NOTES

FACILITIES AND CARE

Many riders have the dream of owning their own horse(s) some day. Horse selection and ownership involve many considerations. Taking riding lessons, helping out with a friend's horse, working in exchange for riding lessons, and leasing a horse are all ways to get experience with horses without actually owning one. The most satisfactory ownership experience should come with maximum knowledge and preparation ahead about the routine needs of the horse.

Commitment

Horses are a 365-days-a-year commitment. Going away on vacation requires you to hire or trade off with someone responsible who can provide daily care while watching for behaviors that may indicate illness or lameness. Horses frequently live for twenty or thirty years and often become like members of owners' families. Horse ownership should not be entered into without due consideration.

Leasing or sharing a horse or helping with another person's horse is a good way to determine whether horse ownership is for you. Such agreements should be put in writing to ensure the horse is cared for properly and the handlers understand what duties and payments are their responsibility.

While we are not always able to predict our future, we can guess at life changes that may occur. Moves or changes in lifestyle may cause us to need to find a new home for our horses. Finding a good home can be challenging and takes time. Turning the horse out to pasture to fend for itself is not a suitable solution, and giving a horse away does not assure the animal good care. Most horse enthusiasts prefer to keep an old favorite horse around, increasing the animal's care as needed to keep it comfortable, and consider euthanasia when the horse is no longer comfortable.

Costs and Requirements of Ownership

The purchase price of the horse is small in relation to the cost of ownership. While the most expensive care is not necessary, certain minimum standards of care are considered essential.

Veterinary care. Routine care includes inoculations against disease and checking (possibly floating) the teeth. Disease prevention also includes isolating new horses from others on the property and preventing the spread of disease between horses. Conditions like colic (digestive system upset, which is potentially fatal) and founder (metabolic imbalances often causing lameness) can often be prevented by good management practices. First aid can be carried out by the owner under the supervision of the veterinarian.

Grooming. Routine coat care and checking the horse daily for injuries is covered in Chapter 6, Grooming.

Parasite control. Deworming is normally carried out by the owner and includes routine administration of anthelmintics (drugs that kill internal parasites) and control of external parasites (flies, ticks, etc.) both on the animal and in the environment.

Farrier work. Even the barefoot horse needs its hooves trimmed on a regular basis—usually every six weeks. A shod horse will need its shoes reset or new shoes fitted on approximately the same schedule.

Feed and water. Clean water of a comfortable temperature must be available to the horse 24 hours a day (unless the animal is hot from work or is suffering from a malady like choke). The horse must be fed at least twice daily; if on pasture, the horse still must be checked at least daily. Pastures require maintenance, including mowing, fertilizing, and periodic checks for toxic plants.

Exercise. Regular exercise is important to horse health. Access to a paddock or pasture will allow the horse to move around on its own but does not replace conditioning-type exercise. In addition to being the reason you got the horse, riding is an excellent form of exercise for the animal. Other options of varying advantages and disadvantages are ponying, longing, round-pen work, and mechanical horse walking machines. You may be able to ride on your own land or have nearby private or public lands available. Riders generally find that some time in a riding arena is desirable to promote disciplined riding. Trailering the horse to riding areas is enjoyable but can get tedious if it is your only option.

Sanitation. Manure and urine-soaked bedding must be removed from stalls at least daily (twice daily is desirable when the horse lives in the stall). Some type of manure management plan is needed for run-in sheds, paddocks, and pastures (which should be dragged periodically to break up the manure). Accumulated manure should not be spread on in-use pastures because of parasite reinfestation. Other alternatives are composting, spreading on unused land or hayfields, or removal from the property. In some areas of the country, you may be lucky enough to get people to carry it away for free, but often you have to pay to get it hauled away and disposed of. The reaction of neighboring property owners to manure and the flies that commonly accompany it is an important consideration in planning the layout of your facilities.

Record keeping. Records should be kept on horse identification; veterinary, health, and medical work; farrier work; and breeding.

Insurance. You might want to keep your horse insured against mortality and loss of use or for surgical care. Farm insurance is available; if you care for other owners' horses, you may need care/custody and possibly commercial liability insurance.

Education. Continuing education of the horse owner in management practices helps the horse get the best care, and riding education (lessons or clinics) keeps the rider from developing bad habits and allows both the horse and rider to advance.

Facilities

The type and layout of housing facilities vary according to many factors like climate, use of the horses, and how the animals are cared for (by one person at home or by a hired staff responsible for a stable full of horses). In all cases, safety and comfort for horses and handlers, attention to details regarding health (ventilation, flooring, etc.), and efficiency for workers are paramount. Cost efficiency is an important criterion. The site should be selected carefully before building. Fire danger and climate (including weather concerns) must be taken into account.

Horse facilities require constant attention to maintenance details to ensure continued safety and health; these tasks are easy to put off, but problems have a way of increasing or worsening over time unless resolved. The nature of horses—to move about freely, to interact with each other, and to eat forage during most of the day—must be taken into account. For example, box stalls should be large enough for the horse to lie down in comfortably and be designed to be easy to clean. All surfaces with which the horse may have contact (walls, fences, etc.) must be free of obstructions and sharp objects. Fencing should be sturdy, flexible, strong, and visible. Pastures should be divided so that the horse can be contained in a small area when the ground is too muddy or the grass too rich, and several smaller pastures allow rotation, which maximizes grass yield. Do not mistake green growth for edible forage; check often for plants that may be poisonous and to determine when the forage has been grazed down enough to warrant rotation. Mowing is necessary to keep weeds and less desirable forage from taking over.

Fire

Fire in a horse barn, near horse housing, or in the surrounding area (forest, grassland, etc.) is a very real and very serious possibility. Regardless of your setup, you need to have fire-prevention, fire-fighting, and fire-evacuation plans. With attention to safety, most fires can be prevented.

Fire prevention includes storage methods for flammable supplies (stall bedding, hay, tractor fuel, etc.), control methods for flammable materials that accumulate (dust, cobwebs, brush/weeds, etc.), minimizing sources of ignition (smoking devices, sparks from machinery and electrical appliances, etc.), and a facility designed with prevention in mind (including wiring precautions, lightning grounding devices, and plans for heating devices). Fire prevention is an ongoing effort.

Fire-fighting plans include placement of fire-fighting devices, access to water sources, communication with firefighters, and clear routes to the facility for the firefighters. Facility design includes fire-resistant walls between, or separate buildings for, housing and storage areas.

Fire evacuation involves exit routes, safe holding areas at the facility, planned destinations off the facility, horses that will load on trailers in the excitement of an emergency situation, and enough trailer space or plans for repeated trips for all the animals. Parts of the evacuation plans should be practiced with all potential barn workers/horse owners and the horses.

NOTES

APPROACHING, HALTERING, LEADING, AND TYING THE HORSE

As you approach the horse for the first time, it helps to know a little about the animal. The horse's resting habits, instinctive reactions, vision, hearing, and attitude are important to understand. Most experienced horse people do not appear to rush or hurry around horses, although they can be very fast and efficient. Horses are usually most comfortable around people who move smoothly and calmly.

Horses can sleep standing up. The arrangement of bones, ligaments, and tendons in their legs keeps their legs from buckling while they doze. It sometimes takes the horse an instant to become oriented upon awakening, and, especially if the horse is startled awake, it might react instinctively to whatever startled it. To an animal whose ancestors were preyed upon (rather than being predators), the obvious reaction would be to put distance between itself and the perceived threat. When confinement prevents escape (the horse is tied or in a stall), the instinctive defense is to kick. Check to see that the horse is awake before you approach, so you can avoid startling it. Speak to the horse, and it will turn to look at you. Move toward the horse purposefully but not aggressively.

The horse's eyes are placed on either side of the front of its head, enabling the animal to see almost 360 degrees. Particularly when the horse is grazing, a slight turn of its head enables the animal to see you (or anything else) approach from any direction by looking between its own legs.

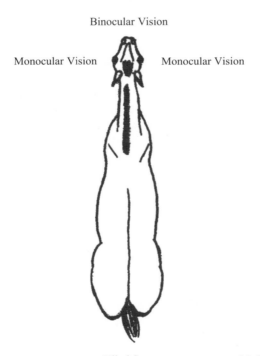

Binocular Vision

Monocular Vision   Monocular Vision

Blind Spot   **5.1 Horse's Field of Vision**

This eye placement means that the horse cannot see directly behind itself unless it turns its head. If something unexpectedly comes into its field of vision (for example, you silently walk up behind the animal where it cannot see you and then move to where the horse catches sight of you out of the corner of its eye), the horse is likely to react instinctively. If you get close enough to touch the animal and it still does not know you are there, your touch might startle it. Try always to approach the horse and work around the animal so that it can see you. If you have to cross the horse's blind spot, speak to the animal or keep a hand on the horse to remind it where you are. This reminder helps the horse keep track of you so it is not surprised when you reappear—whether on the same side or on its other side.

The vision on either side of the horse's head is monocular—one-eyed and without depth perception. This vision is sufficient for detecting predators by seeing movement at a distance, and it is useful in everyday work. For binocular vision that enables the horse to judge distance and depth, the animal focuses forward with both eyes; the area of this vision is limited to the front of the horse's head. By turning its head, the horse can use this vision to observe through a wider area.

To determine what a horse is paying attention to, watch its ears. If one ear is forward and the other is pointed back, the horse is aware of happenings both in front of and behind it. If both ears are forward intently, the animal is using its binocular vision to watch something out in front.

In order to focus on far away objects, the horse raises its head and points its nose. Focusing on close objects requires a lowered head and/or the nose to be brought in some. One theory of focusing is that the horse's retina (back of the eye) surface is ramped (unevenly curved), and the different head angles project the image to one or another part of the retina for clear focus. Regardless, understanding the need to move the horse's head to focus is useful for riders and horse handlers who maneuver horses through trail obstacles, into trailers, over jumps, and around show arenas. Because of the eye placement toward the front of its face, the horse cannot see directly underneath its nose; to look at the ground nearby, the animal will have to lower its head considerably. This head movement is why abrupt rein aids that cause the horse to raise its head are undesirable while the animal is picking its way over a rough spot in the trail.

Focusing Far into the Distance

Focusing on Close Objects

5.2 Horse Head Positions for Eye Focusing—Distance and Close

The horse has acute hearing. Although the animal cannot differentiate between similar words, it can determine meaning from the tone of voice used. A soothing tone of voice will reassure the horse, while a sharp reprimand can be effective discipline. The horse can also distinguish between a number of syllables, the softness or sharpness of the sound, and the rising or falling inflection in your words. When used with a touch on the animal's side or rump, the clicking noise made by some horse enthusiasts will move the horse sideways or forward.

The horse's ears also show the animal's attitude. Interest is shown by one or both ears turning to catch sounds. One or both ears may point backwards to hear as you work beside or behind the horse (do not mistake this position for aggression, which is marked by the ears back flat near the neck).

When a horse is annoyed or being aggressive, the animal may threaten by flattening both ears back against its neck. This threat is usually accompanied by an aggressive turn of the head.

A common source of irritation is another horse that has come too close. Horses establish their own pecking order or hierarchy when they are loose together. When you ride or work around a horse, it is safest to stay clear of other horses.

Some horses will threaten people when they are uncomfortable. A horse that threatens when groomed may be sensitive to the pressure. Groom the animal gently enough that the horse is comfortable. Some horses will threaten people when the girth or cinch is tightened. Always tighten the girth or cinch in such a smooth way that the horse is not uncomfortable. Ask your instructor for help.

Some horses will threaten people when they would rather be left alone (for example, when you walk into their stall to halter them). Horses should not be allowed to threaten people; if you feel the horse is being aggressive toward you, get your instructor to show you how best to handle the situation.

Training

Any time you are working with a horse, you are contributing to its training. This rule applies to every situation, from approaching the animal with a halter in its stall to horse show competitions. Hopefully you are reinforcing the horse's training by consistently presenting cues and rewarding the animal's responses. Rewards include releasing the cue pressure or ceasing the cue as soon as the horse begins a correct response. After a second or two of delay, the relationship of cue, response, and reward are lost to the horse's mind. Giving inconsistent cues and failing to reinforce correct responses can confuse the horse—green horses may lose their training, experienced horses can become less sensitive, and horses with sensitive temperaments can become nervous or irritated. School horses are mostly highly tolerant animals.

Horses that have been reinforced for appropriate behaviors, particularly during a relatively short time by skilled trainers, still need consistent cues and reinforcements to continue their desired behaviors. Horses learn by repetition and become more steady and predictable in their responses as they gain experience in new situations. They are creatures of habit in most every aspect of their lives, and it takes time to establish good habits. Unfortunately, it seems that undesirable habits are relatively quicker and easier to establish than good habits are.

When it is necessary to correct the horse, the correction must be made immediately for the horse to associate its response with your correction. Sometimes discipline is appropriate—a sharp "no!", a slap with your hand, or a flick with the end of your lead rope. At no time should a horse be hit in anger. Sometimes horses can be given something to do when they exhibit inappropriate behavior (for example, a horse that lips at you as if to bite may be asked to step back a few steps), and this practice generally works better than discipline to extinguish the behavior. Your instructor will help you learn to correct the horse in a way that will advance the animal's training.

Do not encourage any dangerous behavior that may reappear at an inappropriate time or become a habit. Behaviors that seem cute in young horses can become more dangerous as the horse gets older and larger—examples are nuzzling, biting, pawing or striking with a front hoof, kicking, and rearing. Even behaviors that seem innocuous (crowding your space, rubbing on you) can be problematic when they turn into stepping on your feet and tearing your shirt with the buckles on their halters. Your instructor will help you identify what is appropriate for the horse to do and what is not.

Approaching the Horse

It is generally preferable to approach your horse from its front and left. It is important that the horse sees and hears you approach. If its hindquarters are toward you, approach the animal at an angle so that the horse can see you. Speak to the horse and watch for its ears to flick in response.

If you approach a horse in a box stall, walk toward its left (preferably) or right shoulder. If the horse is standing in a way that does not allow you to approach it in this manner—for example, the animal is standing with its hindquarters to the door—move the horse around with your voice and a gesture with the tail of your lead rope if necessary. When approaching a horse in a tie stall (narrow stall), look for signs that the animal welcomes your entry before moving between the horse and the wall. If the stall has a butt rope at the back, unfasten it. Never duck under this rope, because when you bend over, you risk getting kicked in the upper body or face.

Place a hand firmly on the horse's neck, shoulder, or hip, and push the animal to the side if necessary. Step toward the horse's shoulder. As you approach its head and extend your hand, the horse should turn toward you and/or allow you to bring its head toward you. While the horse should be comfortable with being touched on the head, patting its face is not usually the best way to become familiar with a new horse.

The safest place to stand when working with a horse is close to its side, between its shoulder and hip. Do not spend any more time than necessary in front of or behind a horse, and when passing behind the animal, either stay a horse's length back or, in a stall, stay close to the horse's hindquarters with your hand on its croup. Horses do not normally kick at people. However, it is always safer to keep in mind that they might. By staying close to the horse's hindquarters as you walk behind it, you would not be in a position to receive the full impact of a kick.

Haltering

Halters often have a buckle on the crown piece (or sometimes one buckle on each side of the crown piece). Approach the horse with this buckle unfastened and the halter held in your left hand by both the buckle strap and the crown piece. Lay the lead rope over either arm. You can stand at the horse's left shoulder and place the lead rope over its neck. With the halter in your left hand and while standing at the animal's left shoulder, reach over (preferably) or under the horse's neck with your right hand. Reaching over the neck allows you more control over the horse's movement than reaching under its neck. If you are otherwise in control of the horse (you have the lead rope around its neck, for example) and its head is too high, you can use gentle pressure and release to get the animal to lower its head. Grasp the crown piece of the halter with your right hand and, guiding the nosepiece with your left hand, pull the halter up over the horse's nose. By making a ring of the noseband, you can raise the halter without dragging it uncomfortably over the horse's nostrils. Raise the halter onto the animal's head. Buckle it so that it hangs with the noseband about two fingers below the horse's cheekbones.

When using a halter with a continuous (or permanently fastened) crown piece (and usually an unsnapped throatlatch), go through the same procedure except that you will have to slide the noseband up onto the horse's nose and then slip the crown piece over its ears. Lay each ear forward from the base in turn while slipping the crown piece back; avoid bending the middle of the ears or dragging them forward under the crown piece. Finally, snap the throat snap.

When using a tied rope halter, use the same procedure. This halter should fit with the throatlatch tucked in behind the horse's jawbones, the noseband comfortably between the point of the cheekbone and the corner of the mouth, and the lead-rope knot close enough to the jaw so as not to catch on protrusions in the barn area or for the horse to catch a forefoot in. The crown-piece knot is tied around the loop, not around the crown-piece rope. See diagram 5.4 for the proper placement of the knot.

While the names for the parts of the halter (and bridle) may seem like just some more terms to remember, they are very logical in their origin: crown piece where a crown would be, throatlatch at the horse's throat, noseband around the animal's nose, and cheek piece along the horse's cheek.

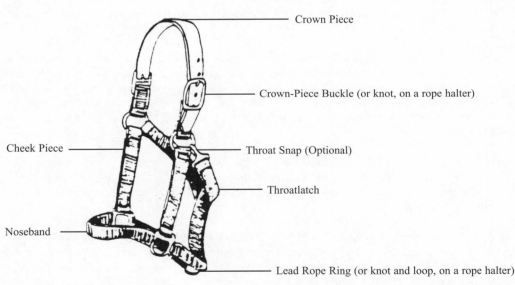

Crown Piece

Crown-Piece Buckle (or knot, on a rope halter)

Cheek Piece

Throat Snap (Optional)

Throatlatch

Noseband

Lead Rope Ring (or knot and loop, on a rope halter)

5.3 Parts of the Halter

24

5.4 Fitting and Tying a Tied Rope Halter

There are a number of quick-release knots; this one works well and is relatively easy to tie. Stand beside the horse; both you and the horse should be facing the post. Allow a short length (one to two feet) of rope between the halter and post (allow for the rope to lengthen while you tie and still be short enough to be safe). Form the knot within a short length of the rope so that when you tighten it, you will have a compact knot. If the horse commonly fiddles with tie knots and you think the animal may untie itself, you can form an additional bend and put that bend through the loop resulting from the first bend. This procedure is sometimes called a daisy chain, and it will delay the horse's efforts to loosen the knot.

1. Pass the free end of the rope around the post and back over itself.
2. Bring the free end toward you, and make a bend.
3. Push the bend down and toward you through the upper part of the loop you have just formed, and pull the bend through.
4. Hold the bend, and push the knot toward the post with your other hand to tighten.

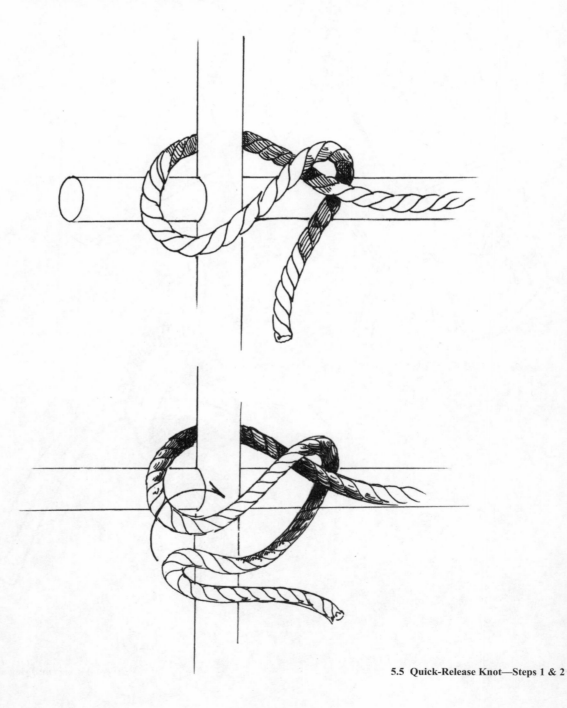

5.5 Quick-Release Knot—Steps 1 & 2

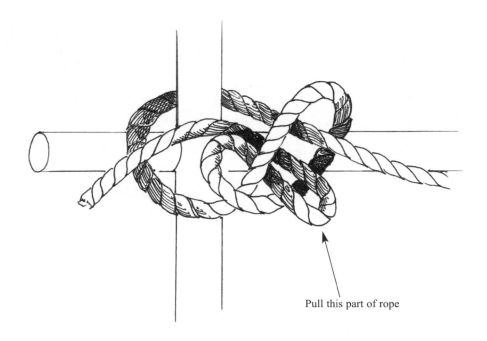

Pull this part of rope

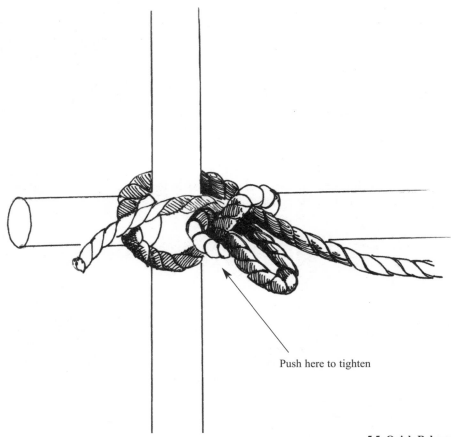

Push here to tighten

5.5 Quick-Release Knot—Steps 3 & 4

27

Leading

Lead the horse by walking on the animal's left side near its neck. Your right hand holds the lead rope (or reins) 6 to 12 inches from the horse's chin; your left hand holds the remaining rope (or reins). Never wrap or coil the rope or reins around your hand, as this practice makes it difficult to let go if necessary. Instead, fold the rope or reins in lengths across your palm and close your fingers around them.

Walk beside the horse and face forward. Keep the horse at arm's length. If the animal hesitates, lead it one step to either side and then forward, or you can gesture with the tail of your long lead rope (check with your instructor for details). Do not stand in the horse's path and pull on the animal; this position leaves the horse without a place to move, and most horses will resist by pulling back.

Remember that the horse is wider than you are. Be sure to open stall doors and gates all the way. Protruding stall door latches are dangerous; push them back, flush with the open door, before leading a horse through. You should always pass through a narrow space ahead of the horse to enable you to stay in control and out of danger. Watch the horse (over your shoulder or turned slightly toward the horse—ask your instructor) as you lead the animal through the obstacle to make sure the horse is clearing it.

Tying

Tie the horse short enough so that it cannot put its head down and get a leg over the rope; depending on the situation, one to two feet of slack works well. Tie the horse to a solid object. Remember that the horse is strong and can pull back hard enough to break weakly constructed fences. A loose animal dragging a tie rail after itself is liable to get hurt. Tie the horse at or preferably above its nose height. This position lessens the horse's leverage if it does try to pull back. Make certain the knotted end of the rope cannot slip down on the object it is tied to. If the knot slides down to the ground, the horse may panic if it suddenly realizes that its head is being held down to the ground.

Use an appropriate knot for the situation. There are different tying philosophies; ask your instructor for the preferred method to tie horses. In general, a quick-release knot is used on horses that stand quietly. Pulling the free end of the rope releases the horse, but only if the animal has not begun to pull back. Once a horse pulls back hard on a quick-release knot, it is difficult to untie the knot. A horse that might pull back may be tied with a bowline knot; this knot will not tighten, so you should be able to untie the horse even after the animal has pulled back hard. In an emergency—for example, the horse has pulled back, fallen, and its neck is at an awkward angle—it is usually impossible to get to the knot safely or to untie it (because of the horse's pressure on it), so horse enthusiasts should carry a sharp pocket knife in case they have to cut a lead rope.

When tying a horse in a stall, stand the animal in a place where you have sufficient room to work comfortably on both sides. Never tie a horse to the stall door; in case of a problem, you cannot get out the door.

Cross tying is a method used to restrain a horse in an open area like an aisle or grooming stall. Two ropes are used instead of one. The ropes are attached about 6 feet high on opposite walls or posts, and they stretch into the center where they attach (preferably with quick-release fastenings) to either side of the horse's halter. Cross tying helps keep the horse in the middle of the working area; this way the groom can work on both sides of the horse easily.

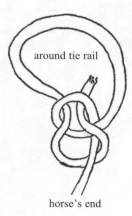

around tie rail

horse's end

1. Pass the free end of the rope around the tie rail.
2. Make a circle in the part of the rope between the horse and the rail, with the horse's end underneath.
3. Pass the free end of the rope up through that circle, either direction around the horse's end, and back down though the circle.
4. Pull snug from all directions.

5.6 Bowline Knot

GROOMING

Good grooming is essential to the health and appearance of all horses, whether they are stabled, exercised, or ridden. The value of grooming is threefold. Grooming cleans the hair and stimulates the pores of the skin. This practice results in cleaner and healthier skin. Vigorous grooming massages the muscles underlying the skin and thus improves their condition or fitness. Grooming also allows you to check for injuries. Even pastured horses that are not ridden should be checked daily for injuries.

A thorough grooming job can take hours or less depending on the speed at which you work and how often the horse is groomed. Extra time spent grooming never hurts, but sometimes you must hurry to complete a lesson and need to do the most important parts well while letting other tasks wait. Your instructor will let you know what degree of turn out (grooming) is expected for lessons.

While grooming, always stay alert and watch what the horse is doing; this practice helps you stay safe. Remember never to kneel (on one or both knees) beside the horse. If you are kneeling, you cannot get away from the horse quickly enough to avoid being kicked or stepped on. Never balance with your hand on the ground; the horse may step on your fingers. Keep your head well away from the animal's legs. Do not put your head in front of or behind its legs; a concussion could result. If you should drop a grooming tool under the horse, either move the animal away before you retrieve it or move the tool out from under (or behind) the horse with your toe. Never lean down and put your head in a dangerous position.

Grooming Equipment

Some of the many popular grooming tools and products are described here, and a few are pictured. A rider can do an excellent job of grooming with these basic tools. There are many additional products and tools available, and most riders enjoy choosing those which they feel do the very best job for their circumstances.

Hoof pick. This tool cleans out the ground surface of the hoof.

Hoof dressing or oil. This preparation is brushed on to the hoof, particularly at the hair line (coronet band), to replace lost moisture, retain hoof pliability, and reduce the incidence of cracks.

Currycomb. The traditional black oval rubber currycomb and a number of newer flexible-toothed grooming tools remove dead hair and bring dust to the surface of the body. There are also a number of smaller currycomb-type tools and grooming mitts available that are ideal for more sensitive areas. The traditional metal currycomb is used only to remove dried mud or sweat when the coat is thick; it is too rough for many horses and for many parts of the body.

Plastic-toothed Sarvis currycomb. This dual-purpose tool may be used to remove mud on the coat or to brush the mane. It should never be used where a long mane is desired and is not recommended for use on the tail, because it can pull and break mane and tail hairs.

Brushes. Three types of brushes are generally used: 1) a stiff-bristled cleaning brush (those made of natural fibers are traditional and popular) for the body and mane/tail; 2) a softer smooth-fiber body brush that will pick up the fine dust and dirt particles left behind by the cleaning brush; and 3) a stiff and sparsely bristled water brush to dip in water and brush the mane down flat against the neck and the tail hairs down at the dock.

Shedding blade/sweat scraper. This tool is handy in the spring to shed out winter hair; the smooth side can be used to remove heavy sweat or excess water (the latter after a bath).

Mane comb. This small metal comb is sometimes used instead of the brush to untangle the mane (but beware—it can break hairs and pull hairs out). A smaller version, which also has smaller teeth, is called a pulling comb. It is used to pull the mane—to pluck out the longer hairs and some of the hairs where the mane is too thick. Using this comb results in a shorter, thinner mane. Pulling the mane is usually necessary on a hunter before the mane can be braided for a show and is common on many western show horses.

Grooming cloth. Most often pieces of towel are used as grooming cloths. Dry cloths are used to dry the sweaty coat of a horse after a workout. Damp cloths are used during initial grooming to clean around the eyes, the nostrils, and muzzle, inside the ears, under the tail, and the sheath of a gelding or bag of a mare. A grooming cloth can be used to give a final polish to the coat after the grooming process. Mitts (dry) or sponges (damp) may substitute.

Clippers or scissors. Trimming the long hairs from the face and lower legs neatens the appearance of the horse, particularly before a competition. An electric animal hair clipper with sharp blades works best. Scissors may be used instead for some areas. Horses that need bug protection and live outdoors will do better with their natural hair; check with your instructor or a mentor for advice.

Shampoo and water. The horse should not be bathed too often, because the hair coat will suffer when the natural oils are lost. However, in warm weather, a complete bath is a good way to remove dirt and dead hair. Use a mild shampoo and rinse very well; soap left in the coat will irritate the skin. If the weather is too cold or a complete bath is not needed, spot washing can be used to remove stains from white legs, etc.

Sweat scraper. This scraper is the stiff, permanently curved tool used both to remove heavy sweat and to remove excess water after a bath.

Grooming box. Grooming tools are easiest to keep track of when kept in a container that is stored—usually in the tack room—when not in use.

Additional Grooming Tools

TOOL	DESCRIPTION	USE

Soft-Bristled Body Brush

Stiff-Bristled Body Brush

Hoof Pick

Water Brush

Rubber Currycomb

Metal Currycomb

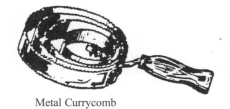

Plastic-Toothed Sarvis Brush

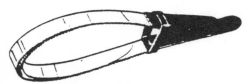

Mane-Pulling Comb

Mane Comb

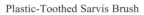

Shedding Blade/Sweat Scraper

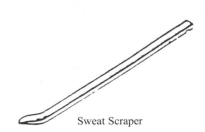

Sweat Scraper

Grooming Tool Box

6.1 Grooming Tools

Parts of the Horse

While most of the labeled parts of the horse are regions of the body, some correspond to bony points (such as points of the buttock and hip and withers) and some are joints (such as knee and hock). Others are bony parts that relate to the nearby joints (such as stifle, shoulder, and elbow). The fetlock is both a joint and the long hair at the back of the joint.

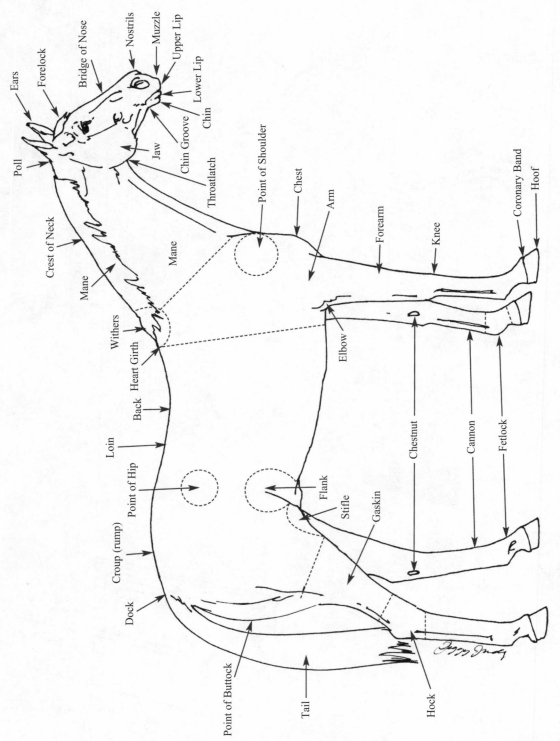

Grooming the Body

The usual procedure is to curry and then brush the body. If the same sequence of body parts is followed each time, you are less likely to miss an area. A practical sequence is head, neck, chest, shoulder, foreleg, back, side, belly, croup, and hind leg. After finishing with one grooming tool on the near side, move to the off side and repeat the sequence.

The currycomb is an excellent tool for removing mud, dirt, loose hair, and saddle marks. Unless the horse is extremely dirty, very longhaired, or thick-skinned, a rubber currycomb is preferred over a metal currycomb. The rubber currycomb is used in a vigorous circular motion over the muscled parts of the horse's body. The rubber currycomb should be used gently if it is needed for the head or from the knees and hocks to the hooves. Clean the currycomb out frequently by striking it on the back of the brush you hold in your other hand (do not use the stall wall and leave a ring mark!). In the spring, heavy winter hair may be removed with either a currycomb or with the shedding blade.

Follow the currycomb with the stiff-bristled brush. A strong, stiffened arm backed up by the weight of your body and vigorous wrist action is necessary to get the hair coat clean. Brush the hair in the direction of its natural lay. Follow the same sequence of body parts as when the currycomb was used. Clean the brush every few strokes by running it over the currycomb that is held in your other hand.

The soft brush may be used next over the entire body to pick up any fine dust or dirt particles missed by the stiff-bristled brush. On a sensitive horse and for finishing touches, the grooming cloth may be used last. In general, use the most effective tool that is comfortable for the horse. This rule will probably limit you to using your hand and/or the grooming cloth on some areas.

The areas most frequently overlooked are also the most critical. Pay special attention to the poll, between the jawbones, elbows, girth area behind the elbows, knees, stifles, hocks, and the backs of the pasterns and heel area. The poll and girth areas are points of friction with the tack; dirt there will cause serious sores. Elbows, knees, stifles, and hocks are body areas that come into contact with the ground when the horse lies down. Caked-on dirt will irritate the skin unnecessarily. A painful fungal infection called scratches, grease heel, or mud fever (resembling scabbed-over cuts) may result from frequently wet pasterns and heels. If you cannot see an area completely while grooming it, feel the area with your hand to make sure it is clean.

Mane and Tail

An adequate job of grooming the mane and tail may be done with a body brush, or (with the consent of your instructor) you can just pick out any bedding with your fingers.

The plastic-toothed Sarvis currycomb is sometimes used on the mane of hunters; it pulls hair out and therefore is not recommended for manes left natural or for the tail.

If you are asked to brush the tail, do it in sections beginning at the ends of the hairs. Hold the main part of the tail in one hand while brushing the free ends with the other. Work progressively toward the dock; this practice allows you to untangle the hairs more easily than starting at the dock and accidentally tightening any knots in the lower ends of the tail. Stand beside the horse and bring the tail around to you rather than standing behind the horse.

The most thorough way to clean and untangle the tail is to wash it. Washing the tail is reserved for special occasions, as it is time-consuming. Additionally, frequent washing will dry the skin of the tail bone. Use mild shampoo worked in well, and rinse the tail very well with clear water (soap residue will irritate the skin, and the horse may rub its tail hairs off while scratching). A conditioner can then be applied according to package directions. Conditioner makes the tangles come out more easily, but it also makes the hair too slick to braid; do not use conditioner above the tail bone on a hunter! After washing the hair, pick out the tangles by hand. Start at the ends and work toward the roots.

Cleaning the Feet

Proper cleaning of the feet will allow you to check for injuries caused by sharp objects, remove stones before they cause bruises, check for secure and properly fitting shoes, and detect thrush. These four points will now be discussed in detail.

Sharp objects (nails, wire, etc.) that puncture the sole may carry bacteria past the hard sole and into the sensitive central area of the hoof, causing an infection. Remove the object only after carefully noting the wound location (and after notifying your instructor); the hole is likely to close up as you remove the foreign object and seal the wound with bacteria inside. The wound opening may need to be enlarged by carving it out with a special hoof knife to facilitate treatment.

Bruises caused by stones may cause lameness and necessitate resting the horse until the bruised sole grows out.

Loose shoes may shift and cause bruises or corns on the sole. A loose shoe is more likely to be pulled off accidentally. The horse may step on the heel of a front shoe with a hind foot. The danger in a shoe being pulled off in this fashion is that chunks of hoof wall may break off, weakening the hoof.

A properly fitting shoe will follow the contour of the outside edge of the horse's hoof. It will be slightly wider (about the width of a dime) than the hoof wall from the quarters to the heels (to allow for hoof expansion as the horse steps down). It will extend at least to the back of the heels of the front and past the back of the heels in the hind hooves. When a shoe has been on for too long, the hoof wall will grow enough that the shoe no longer covers the heels. The shoe heels may be so far forward that they end over the inner buttress, causing pressure and possibly corns. When the shoe no longer fits (or ideally before then) it must be removed by a farrier. The farrier will then trim the hoof wall and shape a new shoe (or possibly use the same shoe if it is not too worn). The shoe is then nailed on. The nails are driven into the hoof wall outside the sensitive area where they do not hurt the horse.

Thrush is an infection of the frog and clefts. It is easily detected by black soggy matter accumulating in the clefts and by the unmistakable (once you have smelled it!) foul odor. Treatment consists of keeping the clefts clean and applying a commercial preparation or dilute Clorox to dry out the area and fight the infection. Prolonged, serious infection may result in lameness.

To pick up the forefoot (the normal cleaning sequence is near fore, near hind, off hind, off fore), stand beside your horse's shoulder facing the animal's haunches. Place the hand nearest the horse on the animal's shoulder and run your other hand down its leg. Grasp the cannon or pastern with your lower hand, and simultaneously push against the horse's shoulder, shifting the animal's weight onto the opposite foreleg. As the hoof comes off the ground, hold it by the hoof wall. You will see people hold the hoof by curling their fingers around onto the ground surface (shoe area); it is safer not to do this if you are inexperienced, because the horse could set its foot down quickly and step on your fingers. While you clean, keep the fetlock joint flexed (bent upward); this position makes it harder for the horse to lean on you. If you hold the hoof with the hand furthest away from the horse, you can also rest that elbow on your thigh to help you balance and hold the hoof up long enough to get the sole and clefts clean. Before setting the foot down, make sure your feet are out of the way!

The hind foot is picked up in much the same fashion, except that as the foot comes off the ground, you take a step to the rear, taking the foot with you. This movement places the hoof out behind the horse, which is comfortable for the animal and will also keep the horse from leaning on you as much.

Remember that the horse's limbs have very limited sideways movement; stay close to the horse instead of pulling the leg sideways toward you.

When cleaning the hoof, the hoof pick is held so that the pointed end points away from you as it protrudes from the heel of your hand. Clean from the heel toward the toe until the entire sole and frog are visible. The dirt must be removed down to the sole and bottom of the clefts; you must learn to clean firmly enough to get the dirt out without unnecessary scraping. Novices often are too gentle; it is good to be careful, but the dirt must come out. Pay particular attention to the clefts on either side of the frog and the depression in the frog; these clefts must be cleaned more gently. The more quickly and thoroughly you clean, the less time you have to hold the horse's foot.

Hoof dressing or oil may be applied to the hoof wall and coronet band. A special hoof-dressing brush or a paint brush may be used. Some horse enthusiasts believe that hoof dressing or oil is helpful, and others do not; ask your instructor for directions.

The unshod hoof looks like this. The shoe covers the wall, white line, and the outer part of the buttress.

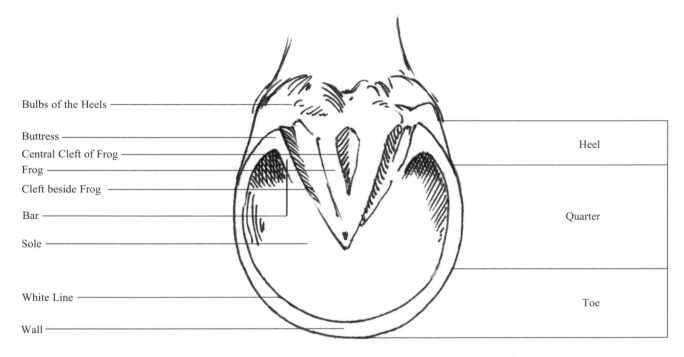

Bulbs of the Heels

Buttress
Central Cleft of Frog
Frog
Cleft beside Frog
Bar
Sole

White Line

Wall

Heel

Quarter

Toe

6.3 Parts of the Ground Surface of the Hoof

Cooling out after Exercise

After moderate exercise, like a riding lesson, take the tack off and find a safe place to put it. The horse will probably be sweaty on its back and neck and between its hind legs.

If the weather is warm, you might want to sponge off the sweaty areas with water. Removing the sticky sweat will allow the hair to dry more quickly. Do not use cold water on the horse's back; cold water can cause muscle cramps. You can use cool water on the areas where the blood circulates near the skin: the chest, the lower neck, and between the hind legs. Cool water will help cool a hot horse out more quickly in hot, humid weather. Use a sweat scraper to remove the excess water; this procedure leaves just a thin film of water that will evaporate and cool the horse while drying more quickly.

In cold weather, if the horse is sweaty, its coat should be rubbed briskly with a towel to partially dry the horse. If the animal is warm or wet, it can be covered with a light blanket, called a cooler, to let the body heat escape slowly and avoid the horse getting chilled. It is important that the horse's hair be dry all the way to the skin in the winter. Walking the horse as it cools out will let the animal's body heat dry the hair.

Walk the horse or allow the animal to graze until the horse has cooled out. It is dangerous to sit on the ground beside a grazing horse; the horse might step on you.

The horse may have a few swallows of water occasionally as it cools out, but the animal should not be given unlimited water until it is cool. The horse's body temperature is determined by how warm its chest feels; the temperature is normal when it returns to what it was before exercise. Even then, if the horse feels slightly warm to you, remember that the animal's normal body temperature averages 100.5 degrees Fahrenheit.

This cooling out procedure also allows the muscles to return to prework condition without stiffening up and is particularly necessary after a hard workout.

NOTES

7

SADDLING THE HORSE

Saddle Styles

The hunter horse, ridden hunt-seat style, wears a hunt-seat saddle. The saddle horse, which might be an American Saddlebred, Arabian, Morgan, etc., is ridden saddle-seat style and wears a flat saddle. The flat saddle may be cut back at the pommel to accommodate the withers of the horse; this saddle is called a cut-back saddle. The stock horse, ridden western style (also called stock-seat style), wears a western saddle. The hunt- and saddle-seat styles are classified as English, as are the saddles.

Preparations

Saddle the horse after you have groomed the animal. The horse should be haltered and tied so the animal stands still for the saddling process. Bridle the horse last so the animal remains tied while you saddle it.

Avoid putting tack on the ground. It is in danger of being stepped on, getting scratched, or collecting dirt.

Approach the horse on its left (near) side, staying in the safer area beside its shoulder.

Saddle Pad

Check the underside of the pad to make sure it is clean. If you are unfamiliar with the pad, look for signs as to which side is the top (it may have leather wear patches there or straps to connect it to the saddle). The underside is usually the softest of the two, if there is a difference.

Place the pad, proper side down, in front of the horse's withers, and slide it back so that the front just covers the withers. It is better to have the pad a little too far forward if you are unsure; you can always slide it back. Never slide a pad forward on the horse's back, because the animal's hair may get ruffled, causing irritation. Make sure the pad hangs down evenly on both sides.

Saddling the Horse and Saddle Fit

Lift the off-side western stirrup and the cinch up over the seat of the saddle; run the English stirrups up the leathers to get them out of the way. Lift the saddle, and place it gently in the middle of the pad. (If the saddle and pad are attached, place them both on the horse together.)

The pommel (English) or fork (western) should sit immediately behind the withers. (Flat saddles on Saddlebred horses will sit back farther on the horse than the hunt and western saddles do.) The tree (foundation) of the saddle is designed so that protrusions below the pommel/fork fit on either side of and behind the withers. They keep the saddle from slipping to either side. If the saddle is too far back behind the withers, it may slip sideways and will not help you keep your weight forward where the horse can most easily carry you. If the saddle is too far forward, it could be uncomfortable for the horse's withers, will restrict the animal's shoulder motion, and may tilt so that you slide too far to the rear of the saddle. To check for shoulder clearance, feel for the shoulder (also called shoulder blade or scapula) of the horse (start below and behind the withers) and palpate along its edge. (Watching and feeling while someone walks the horse is helpful, and you can ask your instructor to show you the scapula's margins.) The front-most part of the saddle that is in contact with the horse should rest behind the rear edge of the scapula in its rearmost swing. The drawings in Chaper 12, Position of the Rider, will serve as diagrams of saddle fit, also.

Additional padding may be required. Sometimes two layers of padding are used under the western saddle. With an English saddle, a pad placed under the cantle provides an extra cushion for the horse's back; a pommel pad cushions the withers. In addition to its cushioning effect, additional padding may be chosen for its usefulness in making the saddle sit correctly (level) on the horse's back. If the cantle of the saddle sits too low, extra padding can raise the cantle to keep the rider forward where the individual belongs.

Extra padding is not a cure for a poorly fitting saddle. A saddle that is too narrow (when viewed from the front) will tend to roll sideways on the horse's back and will distribute the pressure of your weight onto too small an area of the animal's back. A saddle that is slightly wide but high enough in the gullet can be helped by an extra pad, but a saddle that is wide and low will sit down on the withers and make a sore there.

Proper fit is seen by an inch or two of air space (or hand space, if the pad is fluffy) between the withers and gullet. As you put the saddle on, push the pad up into the gullet; this peak may or may not stay while you ride, but making it now helps keep the pad from rubbing the withers and is a good way to check for clearance. The space must remain even with your weight in the saddle; you must check for clearance again after you mount.

Saddle fit is an interesting and complex subject that can be explored further with your instructor if you choose. In the meantime, check the fit criteria described in this text and ask your instructor if you have any questions.

English Pad Attachment

The English pad may have some way to attach it to the saddle; this attachment primarily keeps the pad from slipping back under the saddle. Look for two straps, one on either side, that attach to the billets. Loop them around the most rearward billet that they will reach. There are other methods of pad attachment, like hook-and-loop fasteners on straps that go over the bottom flap (under the billets) or a pocket in the pad for the lower flap of the saddle.

English Girth

Attach the girth to the right-side saddle billets first. The girth has two buckles that attach either to the first and second (from the front) or first and third billet straps. A common mistake of the novice rider is to put the billet through the buckle in the wrong place. The billet belongs immediately under the top of the buckle, not under the support crosspiece. Lift the flap extra high, and check for loose stitching where the billet straps attach to the saddle. Check for tearing leather. Never use an insecure billet strap; have it repaired. A weak billet could cause a serious accident.

There are a number of different types of girths, and they can be made of a variety of materials. Some of the most common types of girths and the materials used are shown in diagram 7.4. An elastic insert near the buckles on one or both ends of the girth will make the girth more comfortable for the horse. The elastic allows the horse some freedom to expand its rib cage as it breathes.

If there is elastic on only one side of the girth, it is traditionally put on the horse's left side to make the final girth tightening easier. If there is a smoother side of the girth (like in the three fold), it goes toward the front (toward the horse's elbows). Other types of girths do not have a specific front edge and can be used with either end on either side of the horse.

After you have attached the girth to two of the billet straps on one side, move to the other side of the horse. As you reach under the horse to find the girth, run your hand across the horse's sternum (immediately behind its chest) and behind the horse's elbows. This procedure is a good final check to make sure you did not miss any dirt in this part of the girth area while you were grooming. As you bring the girth up into contact with the animal's body, be careful not to ruffle the horse's hair by sliding the girth forward. Attach the girth to the same (first and second or first and third) billets as you did on the off side. Pull it up just snug; tighten it later before you get on.

Girths for hunt-seat saddles. Pictured in diagram 7.4, the balding and chafeless girths are shaped to minimize chafing behind the horse's elbows. The three-fold girth's fold should be placed closest to the horse's elbows to avoid pinching loose skin or pulling hair with the open side of the girth. There are many variations on these girths in many natural and synthetic materials.

Flat-saddle girths. Girths for flat saddles often have a flexible attachment for the buckles; these girths are called humane girths. The buckles are purposely buckled at different heights on the billets (the front one high and the rear one lower) to make room for the rider's knee. When the tightening process is complete, the end of the front billet is slipped under the girth strap attached to the rear billet to keep it from showing in front of the flap.

Western Cinch

The cinch usually stays attached to the offside billet or latigo strap between rides. Keep it up over the seat of the saddle while you put the saddle on the horse, and then go around to the off side and bring it down. Avoid letting it fall down so that it strikes the horse on the animal's right side. Be sure it is hanging straight down, without twists. Check to make sure the cinch ring is buckled high enough on the billet or that the latigo is adjusted short enough so that the ring does not end up right behind the horse's elbow (this position often causes rubbing).

Back on the left side, reach under the horse to find the cinch. As you pull the cinch toward you, run your hand across the horse's cinch area (immediately behind the horse's elbows and on its sternum). This procedure is a good final check to make sure you did not miss any dirt there while you were grooming. As you bring the cinch up in contact with the horse's body, be careful not to slide it forward (which roughs up the hair).

Run the end of the near side latigo down through (from inside to outside) the cinch ring, up, and away from you into the saddle dee ring, and repeat the wrap. The knot is made by taking the latigo out from one side of the dee, across in front of the wrapped latigo, and, from the lower side, back up under the dee. Then the end of the latigo is inserted down between the front loop and the wrap, and pulled snug. Instead of a knot, some latigos buckle; the buckle tongue on the cinch ring is used through the latigo.

Tighten the latigo with the knot loose by working the wraps gradually tighter. Leave the cinch snug but not tight; wait until you are ready to mount to tighten it the rest of the way.

If your saddle has a flank (back) cinch, fasten it after securing the front cinch. Always unfasten the flank cinch first when removing the saddle. This practice is a safety measure; if only the back cinch were fastened and the saddle slipped, it would hang around the horse's flank and would likely cause both damage to the saddle and a bad experience for the horse.

Adjust the flank cinch with an inch of slack—enough to allow for breathing but not to let a hoof catch on it. The keeper strap between the cinches must be in place and be long enough to allow the flank cinch to hang nearly vertical. Without a keeper strap or with the keeper strap too long, the flank cinch could slip back and irritate the horse; it could even cause the horse to buck. The keeper strap must not loop downward where it could trap a hind hoof if the horse kicked at a fly.

The cut-back flat saddle is an example of the flat saddles used on horses ridden saddle seat. Flat saddles lack the knee rolls of the hunt-seat saddle, but the other parts are named the same. Note that the front of the flap is cut straight down, there is an indentation in the pommel (it is cut back), and that the seat is relatively flat compared to the hunter's saddle.

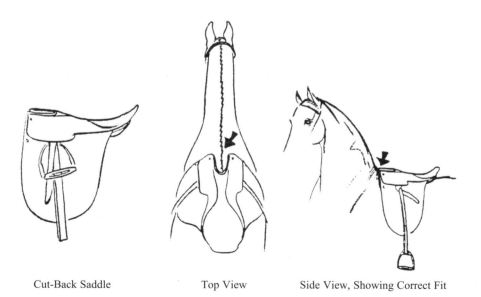

Cut-Back Saddle   Top View   Side View, Showing Correct Fit

7.1 The Cut-Back Flat Saddle

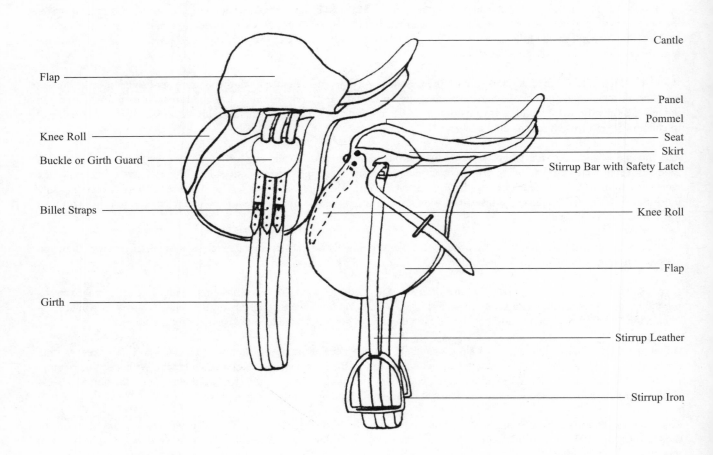

Flap

Knee Roll

Buckle or Girth Guard

Billet Straps

Girth

Cantle

Panel

Pommel

Seat

Skirt

Stirrup Bar with Safety Latch

Knee Roll

Flap

Stirrup Leather

Stirrup Iron

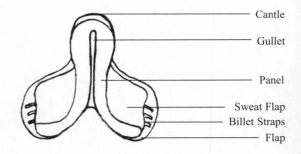

Cantle

Gullet

Panel

Sweat Flap

Billet Straps

Flap

7.2 Parts of the Hunt-Seat Saddle

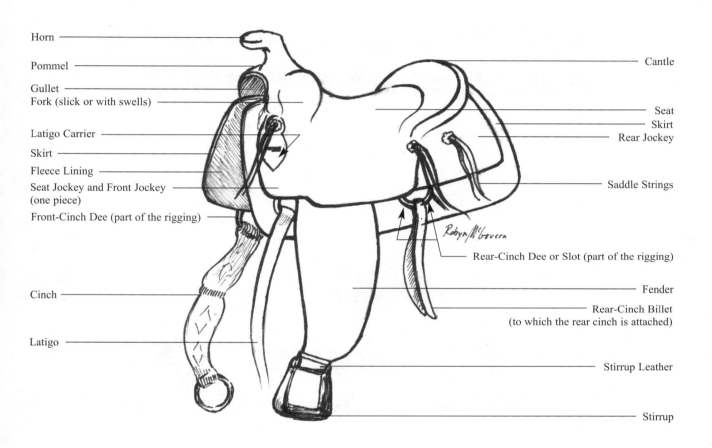

Horn

Pommel

Gullet
Fork (slick or with swells)

Latigo Carrier

Skirt

Fleece Lining

Seat Jockey and Front Jockey
(one piece)

Front-Cinch Dee (part of the rigging)

Cinch

Latigo

Cantle

Seat
Skirt
Rear Jockey

Saddle Strings

Rear-Cinch Dee or Slot (part of the rigging)

Fender

Rear-Cinch Billet
(to which the rear cinch is attached)

Stirrup Leather

Stirrup

Robyn McGovern

7.3 Parts of the Western Saddle

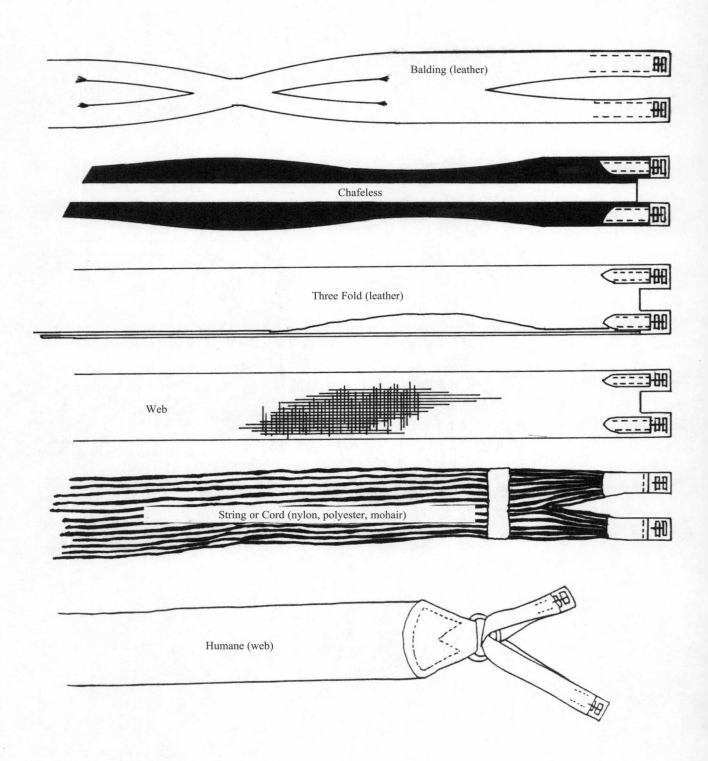

Balding (leather)

Chafeless

Three Fold (leather)

Web

String or Cord (nylon, polyester, mohair)

Humane (web)

English Stirrups

During this whole procedure, the stirrups should stay "run up" the underneath length of stirrup leather, with the long loop of stirrup leather inserted down through the stirrup iron. This position keeps the stirrup out of the way. In fact, whenever you are not sitting in the saddle, English stirrups must be run up the leathers. This practice is an important safety measure. Dangling stirrup irons are likely to get caught on objects, and it is even possible a horse could catch part of its bridle on one if the horse reaches for a fly. If an iron gets caught, the horse will feel the pressure, think it is trapped, and may panic and injure itself or you or damage the tack.

The stirrup safety bar under the skirt should be down (open), so the stirrup leather will come off the saddle in an emergency.

Safety Stirrups

The Peacock safety stirrup pictured in diagram 7.5 is designed to free the rider's foot if it should be caught during a fall. This stirrup prevents the rider being dragged by the horse if the horse does not stop. The thick rubber band is held in place by a leather loop. These stirrups are more traditional on hunt saddles, but work just as well on flat saddles.

Other English safety stirrups are available. One type has curved side pieces. Western safety stirrups that break away and another version that includes the side next to the horse and the tread but is made without most of the outside piece are also available.

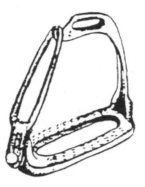

7.5 Peacock Safety Stirrup

Fastening Any Accessories

English and western breast plates, martingales, and tie downs should be fastened after the saddle is fastened and taken off first when unsaddling. If instead the accessories are fastened first and unfastened last, there is a time when the saddle is not secured but is attached to the horse's neck; in an emergency, it is usually better for the saddle to fall completely off than to hang around the horse's neck and down in front of its forelegs.

Tightening the Saddle

When you put the saddle on, the girth/cinch is tightened just enough to keep the saddle in place. This procedure is particularly important if the horse is to stand in the stall for a while, but just as important if you are about to lead the horse out to be mounted. Gradual tightening is more comfortable for the horse. If the saddle is tightened too suddenly or too tightly at any time in the horse's life, but particularly during the early phases of training, the horse can get into a pattern of reacting violently to the cinch being tightened. A horse that reacts in such a way is called cinchy or cinch sour and can be dangerous to itself, to the rider, and to the equipment. It is far better to take the time and sensitivity to prevent this problem.

The girth/cinch buckles/rings should end up approximately the same height on both sides of the horse when the final tightening is complete. In the case of the girth, the buckles should be on nearly the same billet holes on each side. If there is a great deal of tightening to do on an English saddle, some tightening should be done on each side so the horse's skin is not pulled to one side and so that the pressure is even.

Particularly if the horse has a long winter coat, take care that the hair is not caught in the girth or latigo. Make it part of your routine to slide your fingers under the girth or latigo up near the pad and then slide them down toward the elbow. This practice confirms that there are no hairs caught and removes any hair before it gets pulled and causes discomfort to the horse.

Tighten the girth/cinch the rest of the way after you have led the horse to the mounting area. To check the tightness, slip a few fingers under the girth/latigo. Slide your fingers in from the front to keep the hair smooth and stay up near the pad. If you feel down lower near the elbow, the natural depression there will give you a false sense of looseness.

The girth/cinch is tight enough when you feel resistance as you slide your fingers under it. It is too tight if you cannot get any fingers under it at all. It is too loose if you can get your fingers under easily or if your whole hand fits. When in doubt, ask your instructor.

Remember that the saddle tree is made to fit around behind the horse's withers. This placement, along with your balance, helps keep the saddle even on the horse's back. If you sit unevenly in the saddle with more weight in one stirrup, you can make the saddle uneven on the horse's back no matter how tight the cinch or girth is. Horses with high withers do not require as snug a girth/cinch as those with low withers.

Stretching the Forelegs

Your instructor may want you to stretch the horse's forelegs after the final tightening of the girth or cinch. This procedure is particularly important if the horse has a long winter coat, a lot of loose skin behind its elbows, sensitive skin, or a tendency toward girth/cinch sores.

Lift a front foot, as you do when cleaning it. Continue to hold the hoof wall with the hand farthest from the horse (your right hand if you are stretching the horse's left leg), and grasp the knee with the other hand (the one closest to the horse's knee). Lift up the knee until the foreleg is horizontal, and gently pull the leg forward. This procedure pulls the loose skin behind the elbow forward so it does not get rubbed by the girth. Stretch the other foreleg the same way. Be sure to hold on to the reins at all times, and stay out of the way of the horse's foreleg.

Remember to check your girth/cinch again after mounting and/or after walking for a few minutes. Sitting down on the saddle compresses the padding and may make the girth/cinch too loose. The horse may have expanded its rib cage to prevent your tightening the girth/cinch, and after walking around, the horse will have relaxed. If the western cinch is too loose, dismount and tighten it. The English girth, however, can be tightened from the horse.

Tightening the Girth While Mounted

When riding English style, you can tighten the girth as you sit in the saddle. Lift your leg on the side you want to tighten and place it in front of the saddle. Keeping your foot in the stirrup will allow you to regain your balance quickly if necessary. Remember always that an unusual sound or movement anywhere in the area could startle your horse and cause the animal to move suddenly. Raise the flap, hold a billet strap, and guide the buckle tongue into the next hole with your first finger as you pull up on the billet strap. Repeat this procedure with the remaining buckle. Smooth the girth guard down over the buckles to protect the flap from being rubbed by the buckles. Finish by rechecking the tightness of the girth below the flap. If the girth needs to be tightened more than one hole, try to keep the buckles the same height on both sides by tightening each side a hole or two. Remember to leave the front buckle higher than the rear on the flat saddle.

8

BRIDLING THE HORSE

Organizing the Bridle

As with the halter, the names for the parts of the bridle mostly match the corresponding parts of the horse's head.

The first task is making sense out of all those straps! Hold the bridle up in front of you so you can see how it will look when it is on the horse. Hold the crown piece (and thinner noseband or cavesson strap, if English) in one hand and let the rest of the headstall, the bit, and the reins hang down. Make the brow band (if there is one) point toward the front of the horse or the chin strap or chain point rearward (western). Be sure the cheek pieces and cavesson or noseband, if there is one, hang untwisted. Then hold the reins up out of the way as you approach the horse on its left side and stand near its neck.

Maneuvering the Bridle and Horse

Stay out of the way of the horse's head in case the animal moves it sideways. If its head is low, stay to the side so as not to get hit if the horse raises its head suddenly.

If the horse stands quietly, unhalter it and slip the reins back over its head onto its neck (English) or over its neck (western). If more control is needed, the halter can instead be undone and rebuckled around the horse's neck; the lead rope must be untied before moving the halter as a safety measure in case the horse should try to pull back.

Sometimes the horse will be particularly predictable and well mannered about being bridled and hold its head at a comfortable level for you. In this case, you may hold the crown piece at the horse's ears with your right hand and guide the bit into the animal's mouth with your left hand.

Alternately, particularly if the horse is tall, you can hold the headstall, midway down, in your right hand and suspend the bit in front of the animal's lips. The brow band still faces forward; the chin strap is to the rear. To get in this position, slip your right hand under the horse's jaw and then up around the right side of its face, and place your hand firmly on the bridge of the horse's nose. (Among other methods, the reliable one is depicted in the illustration.) This position puts the horse's jaw against your right shoulder.

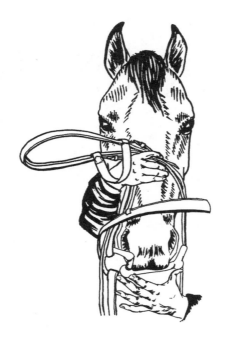

8.1 Holding the Bridle

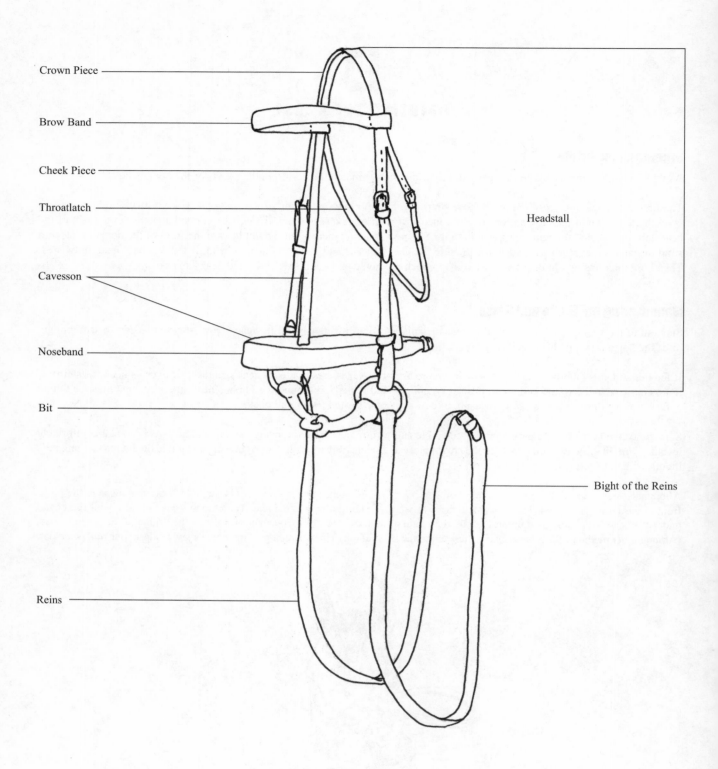

Crown Piece

Brow Band

Cheek Piece

Throatlatch

Cavesson

Noseband

Bit

Reins

Headstall

Bight of the Reins

8.2 Parts of the Snaffle Bridle

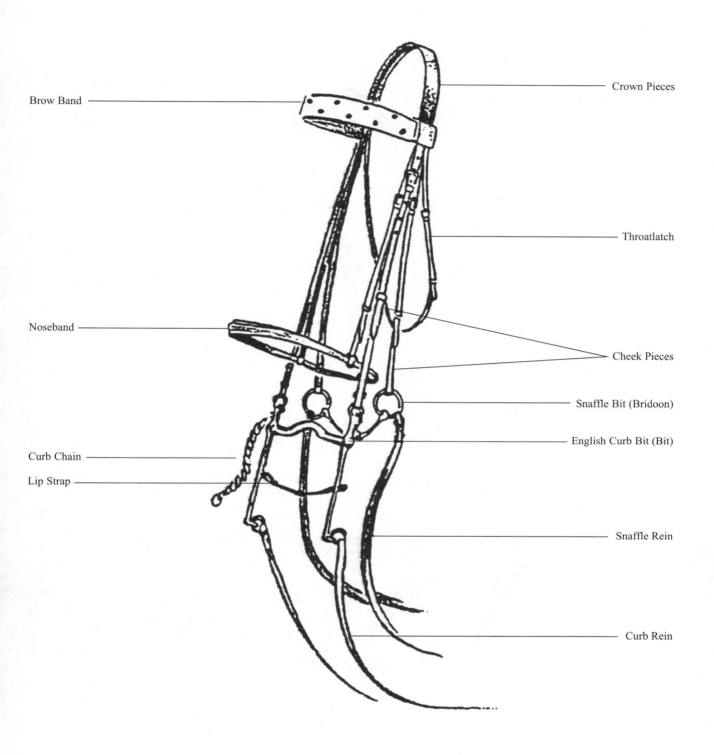

Brow Band

Crown Pieces

Throatlatch

Noseband

Cheek Pieces

Snaffle Bit (Bridoon)

English Curb Bit (Bit)

Curb Chain

Lip Strap

Snaffle Rein

Curb Rein

8.3 Parts of the Double Bridle

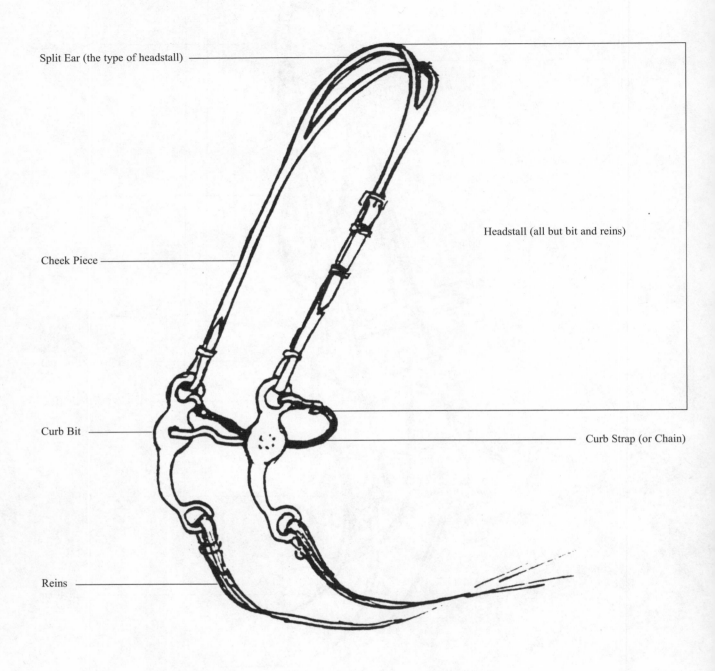

Split Ear (the type of headstall)

Headstall (all but bit and reins)

Cheek Piece

Curb Bit

Curb Strap (or Chain)

Reins

8.4 Parts of the Western Curb Bridle

48

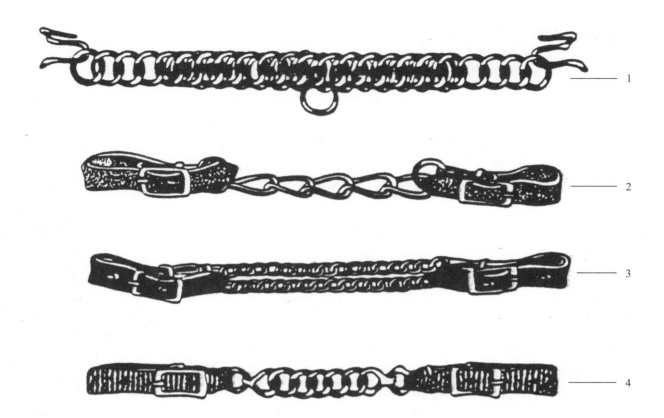

1. English-Type Chain for Pelham and Double Bridle (note center ring for lip strap)
2. Western-Style Leather Strap with Large Single-Link Chain
3. Western-Style Leather Strap and Double Chain
4. Western-Style Nylon Strap and Single-Link Chain

8.5 Curb Chains

While you cannot force the horse to keep its head down, this position will help keep the horse's head within reach. If the horse keeps its head in place, decrease the pressure on the animal's nose; if the horse raises its head, increase the pressure until the animal moves to lower its head, and then decrease the pressure as its reward. Repeatedly asking the horse to reposition its head downward will eventually get the horse to cooperatively move and keep its head within your easy reach. As your timing and anticipation of the horse's movements improves, you can lighten your touch; the weight of a finger on the horse's nose may be enough to bring its head down, and then the touch is removed, but the hand is left nearby in case it is needed as a reminder. If you get the horse to hold its head vertically, it is much easier to slip the bit in without hitting the horse in the teeth.

Use the palm of your left hand to maneuver the bit in between the horse's lips and feel the bit rest against the animal's incisor teeth. Do not bump the horse in the teeth with the bit; this method is understandably uncomfortable and will result in the horse being less cooperative next time. Also, avoid getting your fingers between the horse's teeth!

If the horse does not open its mouth so you can get the bit between its teeth, you may have to slip your left thumb in the corner of its mouth (the left side is most convenient) where the horse has no teeth. If this procedure does not prompt the horse to open its teeth, you might poke the animal gently in the tongue. Another alternative is to press the horse's lip against a tooth. You are trying to make it uncomfortable for the horse to keep its teeth closed; be sure not to make the animal so uncomfortable that it pulls its head away! As soon as the horse moves to open its mouth, remove your thumb or decrease the pressure. Reapply if needed. Be patient. If the horse has learned to close its teeth or raise its head, it may be because bridling has been unpleasant for the animal in the past, and so it is even more important for you to do a good job now.

The Double Bridle

Known as the show bridle if used on walk-trot and five-gaited horses, this bridle is also called a double bridle, bit and bridoon (for the two bits), or Weymouth.

The bridling process is much the same as with a single-bit bridle. However, the curb chain is left hanging by the off-side curb hook during bridling, and both bits are taken by the horse at once. The snaffle is positioned above and behind the curb.

Putting the Headstall in Place

Gently, smoothly, and quickly pull up on the right hand to raise the bit in the horse's mouth. Avoid hitting the horse in the teeth with the bit. The more vertical the animal's head is, the easier it is to do this procedure. Transferring the left hand to the crown piece, keep a gentle upward pressure so the bit does not drop back out. Gently flatten each ear in turn, forward from its base, and slip the crown piece(s) over it. Do not bend the ears or force them under the headstall; this method is uncomfortable for the horse. Rearrange the forelock (and mane if there is no bridle path) neatly. Check to make sure that all the straps on both sides of the horse's head are lying flat. The throatlatch should hang free on the right side, and the noseband/cavesson (English) should be positioned inside the cheek pieces. You are ready to adjust the bridle.

Unbridling

Unfasten the straps and buckles in the reverse order of bridling. Hold the horse with the reins over or around its neck or with the halter around its neck and the lead rope hung over your arm (never tied).

To unbridle, ask the horse to lower its head and hold it near vertical. This head position makes it much easier to unbridle safely without making the horse uncomfortable; it is easier not to hit the horse's teeth, because they are not in the way. Slip the headstall off the ears, but do not let the cheek pieces loop loosely; hold the bit up with the headstall hand. If you instead let the cheek pieces loose and the horse opens its mouth, the animal may get bumped in the teeth with the bit as it exits. Wait until the horse opens its mouth, and then you can work with the animal to let the bit slip out of its mouth. The lowered head and vertical position is particularly important with a curb bit. Holding the headstall up is likewise vital. If you pull the headstall down and forward, it rotates the curb bit in the horse's mouth and causes the curb strap to catch on the animal's chin. The horse can get hit in the teeth, plus the bit can get caught on the animal's incisors or canines and will not drop out. This possibility is emphasized, because once the horse is hurt or scared by the bit, the animal will be that much harder to bridle, and it will be that much easier for you to accidentally hurt the horse again. Keep contact with the horse's head at all times during unbridling.

ADJUSTING THE BRIDLE

After the bridle has been slipped onto the horse's head, it must be adjusted so that it fits properly. A good fit assures comfort for the horse and correct function of each part of the bridle, including the bit.

Safety

Stand in a safe place while you make adjustments. You are safer on one side or the other; if you stand directly in front of the horse's head, you may get hit if the animal tosses its head. Stay far enough away that the horse does not hit you if it swings its head to the side.

The Bit

The first step is to make the bit even in the horse's mouth by shifting the whole headstall to one side or the other. The headstall will move from side to side behind the horse's ears on top of its head. If you do this step without adjusting any buckles, you may find that the bridle fits (the bit is the correct height) already. However, never take correct initial fit for granted!

Check the height of the bit in the horse's mouth. Bit fit philosophies vary, but generally the correct fit is when the bars of the bit mouthpiece are lightly in contact with the corners of the horse's mouth; when you put gentle pressure down (toward the incisor teeth) on the sides of the bit, the mouthpiece will fit just up into the corners without either stretching the lips tight (and possibly making lots of wrinkles) or coming away from the corners of the lips. Some riders determine the correct fit by the number of wrinkles in the corner of the horse's mouth. This method does not always provide a good estimate because of the differences in lip pliability between horses.

The double bridle should fit with the snaffle up in the corners of the mouth and the curb mouthpiece hanging just below it. The bits have separate cheek pieces, so their height may be adjusted independently.

Any faulty adjustment (too low or too high) will lessen the bit's effectiveness as an aid. Too low an adjustment lets the snaffle bit's joint hang down too far on the tongue, encouraging the horse to fuss with the bit and possibly get its tongue over it (which may become a bad habit). Too low a curb-bit adjustment decreases the effectiveness; the bit must stay up near the corner of the mouth to pivot correctly when the reins are applied. Too high (tight) an adjustment puts unnecessary pressure on the horse's lips. Ask your instructor to check your adjustment if you have any questions.

When height adjustment is necessary, use the cheekpiece buckles on both sides or adjust the one buckle and slide the headstall around; make sure you finish with the bit even in the horse's mouth.

On western bridles with the one earpiece, make sure the headstall is also adjusted so that the opening fits around the base of the ear without pinching. The single earpiece should go over the horse's right ear.

The bit will rest on the tongue (see diagram 9.1). It fits in the toothless area between the horse's twelve (six upper, six lower) incisors and twenty-four (twelve top and twelve bottom) molars. This expanse of gums is called the bars of the mouth. Male horses often have one to four canine teeth on the bars, but these teeth usually do not interfere with the bit. Wolf teeth sometimes grow in immediately in front of the molars; these teeth do sometimes interfere with the bit. Wolf teeth have shallow roots and so can be easily loosened; they can become uncomfortable for the horse when the bit comes into contact with them. They are often pulled, sometimes even as a preventative measure before the horse ever wears a bit.

English Noseband or Cavesson

The terms "noseband" and "cavesson" are synonyms to some riders, while others consider them to be different. Those in the latter category do not always agree, but generally the wide, single band around the nose hung by a strap threaded through the nosepiece is a "cavesson," while "nosebands" have a metal ring on each side of the nosepiece. In this context, cavessons are traditional for hunters, while nosebands may be seen on jumpers, dressage horses, and horses ridden saddle seat.

Make the noseband/cavesson even by pulling gently on the upper straps. Hold the rest of the bridle at the crown piece-brow band junction so the bit does not become uneven as you move the noseband. Adjust the height of the noseband to two finger widths below the prominent cheekbone on each side of the horse's face. This position will be slightly higher than halfway between the corner of the mouth and the cheekbone. The noseband/cavesson strap has only one adjustment buckle on one side (unlike the cheek pieces), so after raising or lowering the left side, the whole thing must be slid around until the noseband/cavesson is even again.

Buckle the noseband/cavesson around the nose so that two fingers will fit under it. This placement allows for slight chewing movements but still makes for a smooth profile.

View of the lower jaw from inside the mouth. The bars of the snaffle bit rest across the toothless bars of the mouth, supported by the lips. The joint lies across the tongue.

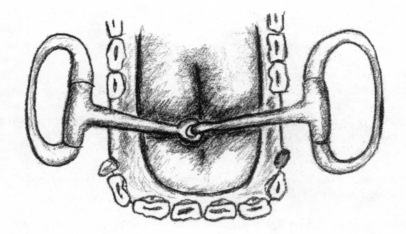

9.1 Snaffle Bit Lying across the Tongue and Bars, Inside View

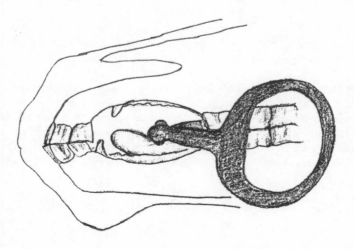

9.2 Snaffle Bit in the Mouth As Seen from the Side

52

Nosebands are sometimes used to keep the horse from opening its mouth when the horse feels rein pressure. A gaping mouth can be minimized by tightening the noseband beyond the snugness described earlier or by switching to another style of noseband. Before taking corrective measures to keep the horse's mouth closed though, it is important to determine that the horse is not uncomfortable from a physical problem like a loose wolf tooth, a poorly fitting bit, or a rider problem, like rough hands.

Examples of nosebands designed to keep the horse's mouth closed around the bit are the drop noseband, flash noseband, and the figure-eight noseband. They fit snugly below the bit in the horse's mouth. If your horse uses one of these, have your instructor show you how to adjust it correctly.

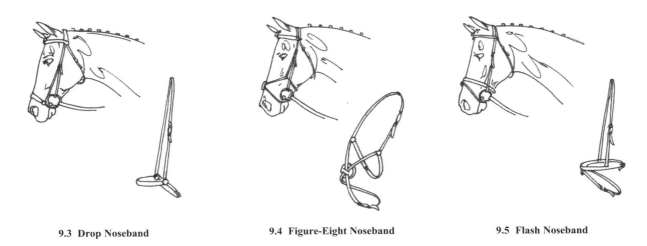

9.3 Drop Noseband   **9.4 Figure-Eight Noseband**   **9.5 Flash Noseband**

English Brow Band

The brow band keeps the crown piece from slipping back toward the rear, down the neck. Check to see that the sides of the brow band lie comfortably at the base of the ears. If the brow band has slid up too high on the horse's head, it will pinch the base of the ears. If it has slid down too far, it will pull the cheek pieces forward, out of place. Sometimes the brow band is made too long and hangs down onto the horse's face. This position keeps it from being effective. Some brow bands will fit too tightly, pulling the cheek pieces forward and irritating the base of the ears. In the latter situation, the brow band must be traded for a longer one (or a different bridle must be used).

Curb Strap and/or Chain

Curb chains are often made of links that must be twisted until they lie flat against each other to form a smooth chain. Curb chains made entirely of chain are attached on the near side by fitting a link over the near side chain hook. There is a special technique to fastening the chain so that it remains flat against the horse's chin groove; it involves hooking the lower (toward the lower shank of the bit) part of a link to the hook instead of the intuitive upper (toward the headstall) part of the link. Ask your instructor to show you how to make the curb strap lie flat. A strap that lies flat is desirable, because it distributes the pressure over the most surface area of the chin groove.

The curb strap (or chain) should be adjusted so that rein pressure brings the shanks of the bit back to a 45-degree angle with the horse's closed lips when the strap or chain contacts the chin.

See diagram 8.5 in Chapter 8, Bridling the Horse, for drawings of common curb chains.

Double-Bridle Curb Chain and Lip Strap

The lip strap on the double bridle is designed to keep the curb chain from rising on the horse's jaw and to keep the bit from turning upside down in the horse's mouth. It is permanently (except for serious cleaning) attached to the chain by a link coming out of the lower edge of the chain. (The curb chain in diagram 8.3 is drawn unattached to the lip strap for clarity in labeling the parts.) The lip strap usually needs no adjustment during bridling.

Throatlatch

The throatlatch keeps the bridle from sliding off over the horse's ears, so it should not be too loose. However, too tight a fit restricts the neck flexion and breathing. Buckle it with about four finger's width of clearance from the deepest recession of the horse's throat (the horse's throatlatch).

Keepers and Runners

All the strap ends should be slid down into the stationary leather loops, called keepers, and movable leather loops, called runners, on the corresponding bridle straps. These leather loops keep the strap ends from flapping on the horse's head as you ride.

BITS AND BITTING

Bits and hackamores come in a variety of sizes and shapes. The right one for any horse is the one in which the horse goes the best, allowing for the rider's ability and the circumstances under which the horse is being ridden. Variations in bits/hackamores will be covered to help the rider understand why a certain bit is chosen for a lesson horse and to allow the horse owner to make an educated choice of bit for a particular horse. The severity of any bit or hackamore depends on how it is used.

The action of any bit/hackamore can be altered by use in combination with nosebands, martingales, and other artificial aids.

There are two main classifications of bits: snaffles and curbs. In addition, the two types are sometimes combined. Hackamores (bitless bridles) come in three main types and are also sometimes combined with snaffle bits.

Snaffle Bits

Snaffle bits are used for English riding and for training of both the western and English horse. Snaffle bits are used in conjunction with English curbs to form double bridles; these snaffles are also called bridoons. With snaffles bits, the pressure you apply is felt by the horse without being multiplied by leverage. Also, direct reining is effective (this type of reining is when the horse is turned by pressure on one side of its mouth). The rider may choose to ride with contact on the horse's mouth; this contact is accepted by the horse without loss of forward motion.

Curb Bits

Curb bits are used when riding more highly trained horses, are traditional for western riders, and are used in conjunction with snaffles for both hunt- and (more often) saddle-seat riding. They work on the principle of leverage: pressure applied by the rider is multiplied and is felt by the horse as coming from more than one direction. These bits act to slow or stop the horse, but not to turn (pressure on one rein is not a clear signal for the horse to turn). The horse must be taught to neck rein—turn away from rein pressure on its neck—before going well in a curb. Consistent contact with the horse's mouth cannot be maintained without slowing the horse's forward motion.

English curbs tend to have straight shanks and loose rings for curb-rein attachment, while western curbs may have fatter, fancy shanks and a solidly attached curb-rein ring. English curbs always have a curb chain, while western ones may have a strap or strap with chain.

Snaffle and Curb Combinations

In advanced stages of training, horses ridden English style may wear a curb and snaffle at the same time. This combination is called a double bridle, weymouth, or bit and bridoon and gives the rider four reins to handle. The rider can use different combinations of pressure for fine-tuning the horse's responses. Horses should only be ridden in this type of bridle when they already are trained to respond to the snaffle bit, and then they receive training in the curb.

Pelham bits have a single mouthpiece but combine curb and snaffle action. They are not as effective as the double bridle in fine-tuning the aids but are still very useful. Pelhams have rings for snaffle-rein attachment near the mouthpiece, plus shanks with places for curb-rein attachment; they have four reins. They may also be used with a converter, a strap connecting the snaffle and curb rings so that one set of reins can be used; this combination is even less effective for fine-tuning the dual action than using four reins, but many horses go well in this tack.

Kimberwick(e)s have D-shaped rings. The reins may be attached in a way that allows them to slide up and down; this type of attachment gives mainly snaffle action. Some Kimberwicks have rein slots in the rings. When the reins are attached to either the upper or lower rein slot, some curb action is applied; the lower slot gives more leverage than the upper. Two or four reins may be used.

The curb chain is like that of the double bridle and pelham. It is adjusted similarly.

Western pelhams, like the Foreman (pictured in diagram 10.1), have attachment places for both snaffle and curb reins. Two or four reins may be used.

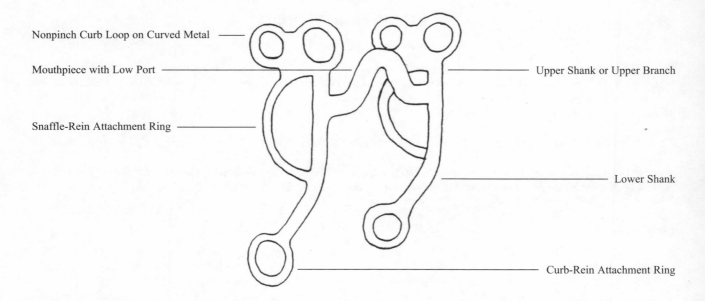

Nonpinch Curb Loop on Curved Metal

Mouthpiece with Low Port — Upper Shank or Upper Branch

Snaffle-Rein Attachment Ring — Lower Shank

— Curb-Rein Attachment Ring

10.1 Foreman Versatile Leverage Bit
Designed by Monte Foreman, this western style pelham has bowed-out upper shanks (also called branches) designed to give plenty of molar and cheek room, plus a curb chain/strap loop set away from the headstall loop and designed not to pinch.

Gag Snaffles and Elevator Bits

Gag snaffles are usually ringed bits that work as snaffles when the reins are applied lightly. Firmer rein pressure causes the bit to rise on the round cheek pieces and puts pressure upwards on the corners of the mouth. They do not have shanks or a curb chain, so they do not give that kind of leverage.

Elevator bits have a lower branch and a similar-length upper branch. The lower branch looks as if it would work as a curb shank, but there is no curb strap (hence, no curb leverage). There may be multiple options for rein attachment on the lower branch. The upper branch (above the mouthpiece) delivers poll pressure when the reins are applied.

Hackamores

These are bitless bridles that act primarily on the horse's nose. They are used successfully on young horses that have not yet carried a bit, on horses whose mouths have been harmed or hardened so that they respond better to a hackamore, and on horses that have become afraid of the bit-insertion or bit-removal parts of the bridling process.

Bosal hackamores have a thick nosepiece that comes together in a heel knot under the horse's jaw. They work by applying pressure to the nose, sides of the nose, or lower jaw area (depending on their use) and are most often used in training green horses. These hackamores are fitted according to the shape and size of the horse's nose and are most often secured with a throat-latch called a fiador. Opening rein aids (where the rider moves a hand out to the side) are clearly recognized by the horse as turning signals; later in training, neck reining may be used.

Side-pull hackamores have a nosepiece that ends in rings—one ring on either side of the horse's nose. A strap around the lower jaw stabilizes the side-pull but does not give curb (leverage) action. This bridle works very much like a snaffle bit in turning and stopping; opening and direct rein aids are effective, and light contact may be maintained. Sometimes these hackamores have snaffle bits attached; the horse feels both nose and mouth pressure.

Mechanical hackamores have nosepieces, shanks to which the reins are attached, and curb chains. Like curb bits, their leverage and the rider's inability to direct/opening rein makes them inappropriate for early training.

Bit Variations

There are many variations on these bits and within the categories of bits. The variations can be generalized to include width of mouthpiece; presence, absence and number of joints in the mouthpiece; diameter of mouthpiece; hard versus cushioned mouthpiece; roughness or smoothness of mouthpiece surface; designs intended to increase salivation; weight; presence or absence of leverage; and shanks or rings outside the horse's mouth.

Width of Mouthpiece

Bits are available in a variety of widths to fit different horses' mouths. The width is the distance, in inches, of the mouthpiece (from ring to ring, cheek piece to cheek piece, etc.). Typical horse width is five inches; ponies or large-headed horses will wear smaller or larger bits, respectively.

Check the fit in the horse's mouth by straightening the joint (if there is one) and watching both corners of the mouth. The width is correct if the bit fits comfortably in the mouth without pinching the sides of the mouth (too narrow) or extending more than a quarter of an inch on either side (too wide).

Too narrow a fit pinches the cheeks against the molars. Too wide a fit will allow the joint of a jointed bit to hang too far down on the tongue and may allow the joint of the bit to bump the upper hard palate of the mouth. It encourages the horse to play with the bit and possibly get its tongue over the bit; it also allows the bit to slide back and forth.

The widths of the upper shanks of the curb bit must allow room for the molars and cheeks of the horse. This dimension is often independent of the mouthpiece fit; the mouthpiece may fit, but the upper branches may be too narrow. Too narrow a fit is very painful for the horse (it presses the horse's cheeks against its molars). Check for clearance here by looking from the front, and replace a narrow-fitting bit or bend (by hand, in a vise, or with a hammer) the upper branches of the shanks outward.

Presence, Absence, and Number of Joints

The mouthpiece may be jointed or not; some mouthpieces have multiple joints. The connection of the mouthpiece to rings, cheeks, or shanks is not considered to be one of these joints.

Joints allow the bit to bend around the tongue when the reins are used; this placement distributes pressure across the tongue and on the corners of the mouth. One joint in the center of the mouthpiece will cause a nutcracker action. The more joints there are, the more the bit conforms to the shape of the tongue and the less nutcracker action there is. The flexibility of the joints differs from one bit design to the next; the more flexible, the more nutcracker or squeezing action there is.

Jointed bits give the horse a slightly different sensation than unjointed bits when just one rein is used; this differencce can be an advantage, but it is mostly personal preference on the part of the rider.

An unjointed bit does not squeeze the tongue. It distributes pressure on the tongue and corners of the mouth if it is a snaffle or on the tongue, lips, and possibly bars of the mouth if it is a curb. Unjointed snaffles are generally used for the most sensitive of horses, often youngsters, because they are mild bits. The functional difference between jointed and unjointed snaffles is that the former allow the rider greater separate communication with one side or the other of the horse's mouth.

Given the definition of a snaffle as a nonleverage bit and noting that snaffles may be jointed or unjointed (or have multiple joints), do not confuse jointed shanked bits with snaffles. There are many jointed curbs in use; they work on the principle of leverage and, hence, are not snaffles according to this definition. Whatever you call it, be sure to understand its action and, therefore, its appropriate use.

An unjointed curb bit may have a port (a hump in the middle) or a straight mouthpiece. The port is designed to relieve some of the pressure on the tongue and transfer that pressure to the lips and possibly the bars. A port high enough to touch the roof of the mouth will encourage the horse to flex at the poll to avoid this pressure; it must be used only on well-trained horses by educated riders. A straight curb mouthpiece without a port acts on the tongue but not the bars.

Diameter of Mouthpiece

There is a great deal of variation in the thickness of the mouthpiece among all types of bits. A thicker mouthpiece distributes the pressure over a wider area and is therefore less severe. A thinner mouthpiece concentrates the pressure on a smaller area and is therefore more severe.

The relative size of the horse's tongue must be considered when choosing a thick mouthpiece. A horse with a relatively thick tongue and/or small mouth may be uncomfortable with a thick mouthpiece, even though it is "less severe." The horse may have too much of a mouthful, or more seriously, the horse may be unable to close its lips over the bit and will get a dry mouth, because its mouth is held open by the thick bit.

The mouthpieces of both bit and bridoon are smaller than those of snaffles or curbs used alone because of the necessity of fitting both bits in the mouth at once.

Hard or Cushioned

Most horses go well in metal bits. However, softer rubber bits are available for more sensitive horses. A metal mouthpiece may be wrapped with leather or latex to cushion it. Extreme care must be taken to not let the covering deteriorate to the point that the horse might swallow pieces of it.

Texture

An infinite variety of mouthpiece textures are available. Textures vary from a milder smooth surface to a more severe rough one. There are many ways to achieve a rough texture. A twisted bit looks like the mouthpiece has been twisted lengthwise, creating ridges that spiral from cheek to cheek. (This bit is sometimes called a slow twist.) The bit may be wrapped with wire (sharp ends must be avoided), or the mouthpiece itself may be two pieces of wire twisted together. The severity can be determined by the feel of the bit across your hand and then imagining the bit in the horse's mouth. Rough-textured bits must be used only by riders with educated hands.

Salivation

A horse with a wet, foamy mouth is usually more relaxed and responsive to the bit than a dry-mouthed horse. Some lubrication is certainly more comfortable for the horse. While salivation is not entirely due to bit design, some bits encourage salivation. Bit variations designed to help establish a wet mouth include copper coating and rollers or keys on the mouthpiece.

Weight

There is some variation in weight between bits, mostly because of size and materials. Changes in weight can affect the height of the horse's head carriage and may be used to advantage in some situations.

Presence or Absence of Leverage

Bits that provide the rider with leverage on the horse's mouth are called curb bits. Curb bits have shanks hanging down outside the mouth to which reins are attached. When pressure is applied with the reins, the horse feels pressure downward on its mouth. Rein pressure also rotates the shanks backward and presses the curb chain or strap against the horse's chin groove. The part of the bit above the mouthpiece rotates forward, putting pressure down on the poll via the cheek pieces (the longer the upper branch, the more potential poll pressure). The horse feels pressure down on its mouth, up on its chin, and down on its poll; by these means, the horse is encouraged to tuck its chin.

Pelhams and other snaffle and curb combination bits have curb-bit action when the curb (lower) reins are used; these reins can be applied independently of the snaffle (upper) reins. When just the snaffle (upper) reins are used, the action is that of a snaffle.

Bits without leverage action are called snaffles.

Shanks

The shanks that characterize a curb bit have already been discussed. There is a significant variation in the lengths of the lower shank and of the upper branch of the shank. Longer shanks and upper branches give the rider more leverage and are therefore potentially more severe. Additionally, the longer the upper branch, the more poll pressure is created.

The curve, or angle, of the shanks to the rear will affect the pressure and its direction. Shanks angled to the rear will lessen the leverage that is possible and are potentially less severe than bits with straight shanks.

The curb bit must hang correctly in the horse's mouth. This placement is a function of the construction of the bit. A test of curb-bit balance is to hold the bit on the flattened palm of your hand and see that it hangs at the same angle as is desirable in the horse's mouth.

The correct adjustment of curb strap or chain is the length that allows the shanks to rotate back to make a 45-degree angle with the mouth when the strap or chain is in contact with the chin groove.

A serious problem with some curb bits is that the headstall and curb strap attach to a single ring on the upper branch of the shank. This attachment puts the curb strap and mouthpiece too close together when rein pressure is applied; they will often pinch the horse's lips between strap and bit. In this case, a better-constructed bit should be substituted (one with separate and separated curb and headstall rings).

Rings

The rings to which the reins of a snaffle bit are attached come in an infinite variety of sizes, flexibilities, and shapes.

Some ring variations are predictable; for example, the bridoon rings are smaller than the rings on snaffles used alone.

A big ring is less likely to get pulled into the horse's mouth when just one rein is used; the same is true with cheeks (the lower or upper and lower pieces outside the mouth that have no rein attachment).

Minor variations in the shape of the rings make little difference in the action of the bit, but these variations reflect the owner's preference. Major variations, like cheek pieces, do affect the action of the bit. Cheek pieces touch the sides of the horse's face and put pressure on one side of the mouth when the other rein is used. They are helpful when teaching inexperienced horses to turn. Single cheek pieces, on the lower side of the ring only, are used in driving bridles (many horses ridden saddle seat are driven also) and as single snaffles for training purposes. The half cheeks keep the bit from being pulled to the side and the ring from getting in the horse's mouth.

The flexibility of the attachment of the ring to the mouthpiece is an important determinant of the amount of play in the bit. A less restricted attachment may encourage the horse to develop a wet mouth. Care must be taken with freely moving rings to ensure that the horse's lips cannot get pinched. This possibility is a particular problem with old bits that have worn so that the junction of joint and ring includes a gap. Rubber bit guards may be used, or the bit must be thrown away.

Severity

Bits work to control horses not because they cause pain, but because the horse has been trained to respond to the bit in a certain way; when the horse responds correctly, the pressure decreases. Training is the key—a horse that does not respond to a mild bit because of lack of training will not respond any better to a stronger one.

The action of the bit is just one of many aids from the rider. When diagnosing bit problems, the whole picture must be scrutinized. For example, if the horse is not stopping, make sure all the aids (including weight and legs) are telling the horse to stop. It is possible that the horse is reacting to another aid (like the rider's bumping legs or forward-leaning upper body) that tells the horse to keep going.

The best bit for the horse is usually the least severe bit to which the animal still responds. Using a mild bit that the horse does not respect is not being kind; it is dangerous. Using too strong a bit will make the horse tense. Creating pain will cause the horse to try to get away from the pain, and the horse may act in ways that are dangerous to both itself and the rider. The ultimate severity of any bit lies in the hands of the rider. A mild bit in abusive hands can cause torture; a strong bit in educated hands can be light and useful.

Named by cheek piece, then mouthpiece
(which are interchangeable):

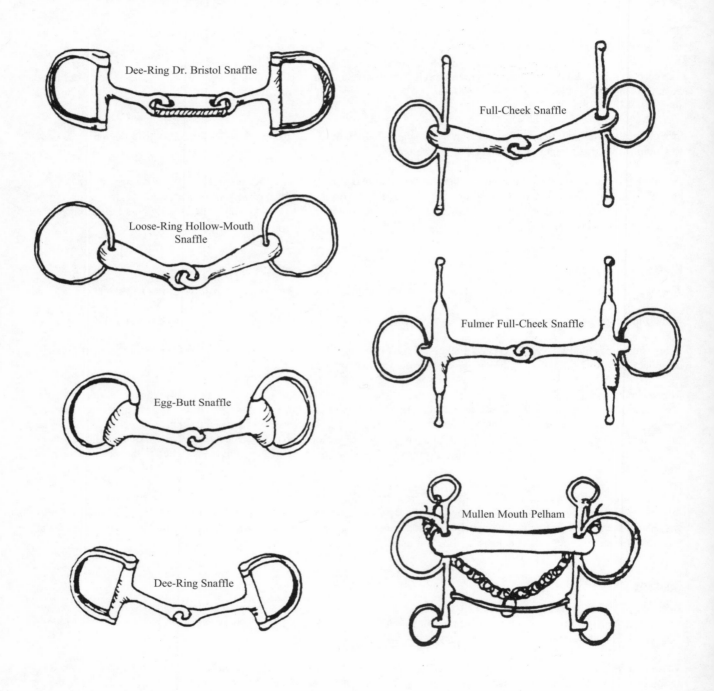

Dee-Ring Dr. Bristol Snaffle

Full-Cheek Snaffle

Loose-Ring Hollow-Mouth
Snaffle

Fulmer Full-Cheek Snaffle

Egg-Butt Snaffle

Mullen Mouth Pelham

Dee-Ring Snaffle

10.2 Common English Bits

English Dee-Ring
Twisted Snaffle

English Half-Cheek Snaffle

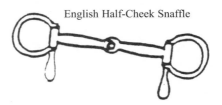

Western Curb (the kind that
pinches the lips)

English Double-Bridle Bits:
English Bit (curb) and Bridoon
(snaffle) (in this case, the snaffle
is a loose-ring snaffle)

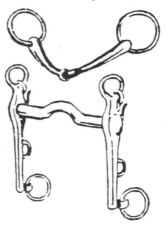

Western Foreman (note
snaffle rings)

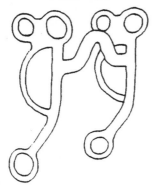

Western Spade (for
well-trained horses)

10.3 Common Bits, English and Western

NOTES

TACK CARE AND CLEANING

The equipment, called tack, used on horses can be expensive to buy, but it will last a long time with proper care. In many cases, it is worthwhile to spend the money for high-quality tack, because it will give years of good service. Tack care is a safety measure also, because strong, pliable leather, strong hardware, and secure stitching are less likely to break at critical times.

Leather

Leather has a natural fat content that makes it pliable and able to support weight and absorb shock. Dried-out leather is stiff and cracks and breaks easily. Leather loses some of its fat content when it gets damp, especially if the dampness is accompanied by dirt, salt, or heat. Prolonged exposure to sun is not good for leather. When mud dries on leather, the mud pulls moisture from the leather. Salt in the horse's sweat removes moisture from the leather as it dries. The heat of an automobile trunk in the summer sun is hard on leather. When dampness is taken out of leather by direct exposure to heat, the leather becomes particularly dry and brittle.

Avoid getting leather wet, if possible. Rain is not always avoidable, but the water used in the cleaning process should be kept to a minimum. The sponge must be wrung out well before cleaning the leather or applying saddle soap. To minimize the effects of moisture, sweat, and dirt, remove sweat and mud soon after riding. If your tack gets rained on, you can remove the excess moisture with a towel and apply a good leather preservative before the leather is completely dry. Let leather dry gradually away from heat sources. If you live in a humid area, you may find your leather mildewing unless you find a temperature- and humidity-controlled environment to keep it in.

Leather has two distinct sides. The flesh side was the underside on the cow (or whatever animal it came from) and is rough in texture. It absorbs oil better than the grain (smooth) side. The grain side was the hair side of the hide. It is more durable, so it is used in areas subject to wear. Wear areas appropriate for grain-side use are the outside of the seat, flap, and fender of saddles and on the inside of English stirrup leathers (where the slicker surface lets the irons slide more easily, too).

Suede

Also known as roughout, suede is leather with the flesh side exposed. Use a wire brush gently to clean and rough up the suede on the seat of a western saddle or knee rolls of an English one. If you use oil or saddle soap on it, it will lose the rough texture. However, in an old saddle with the suede worn smooth, oil can be used to keep the leather from drying and cracking.

Metal Parts

The hardware in high-quality equipment should be strong and not break under pressure. This requirement is one reason to use high-quality tack—the metal hardware tends to be high quality, too.

Corrosion, though, will affect the strength of the best metal. Clean buckles and other hardware, like the safety-release stirrup bar on the English saddle, by removing accumulated dirt. Check for corrosion, and replace badly deteriorated metal parts before they cause an accident. Guard against corrosion in tack stored for a long time by applying a light coat of oil to the metal before storage.

Stitching

Stitching will eventually wear thin or come loose; this damage cannot be prevented, but routine checks can usually keep it from breaking at a critical time.

It is sometimes reported that oils applied to the leather will rot the stitching. This report may be true to a certain extent, but leather is more costly to replace than stitching. Well-cared-for leather can outlast the life of the stitching.

Daily Inspection

When you tack up the horse, inspect your equipment so you can avoid using any dangerously worn equipment. Loose or frayed stitches are a sign that the whole area will come loose soon. Do not trust your safety to loose stitching; have it repaired before it breaks. Pay special attention to the billet attachments to the English saddle, the buckles' attachment to the girth, the latigo, and the headstall and rein ends at the bit. Wherever straps pass around metal, there is the possibility of wear.

Look also for worn or tearing leather, especially at friction points on the billet straps (English or western), latigo, stirrup leathers, and cheek pieces. Notice any corroding or worn metal.

Daily Cleaning

Minimum care after every ride will decrease the work during thorough cleaning (see the section below) and prolong the life of your tack. Any sweat or dirt should be removed from the leather; use either a mild cleaner (there are many good cleaners available) applied with a damp sponge, or use the damp sponge alone followed with an application of saddle soap. (Saddle soap, despite its name, is not a soap but acts instead as a leather sealer and conditioner.) If you rinse the bit immediately after riding, it will be easy to wipe clean; dry it before you put it away.

Thorough Cleaning

Periodic, thorough cleaning is essential to the proper care of tack. This process is time-consuming, but well worth the effort.

Begin by taking the tack completely apart. Often the dirtiest and most worn places are on the inside of folded leather, particularly where it rubs on metal; you must take the tack apart to get to the dirt. The leather that comes in contact with the horse will also be dirty; however, these surfaces will be easier to access.

The English bridle may be fastened to the bit with metal stud fasteners. These fasteners must be undone correctly to avoid unnecessary stress on the leather or studs. Do not pull out on the leather ends. Carefully work the leather until it is free of the stud before sliding the leather out of the keepers.

Drop the bit in your cleaning water. It will be thoroughly soaked and will easily wipe clean when you are done cleaning the leather. Be sure to rinse it off well.

The leather is cleaned with a damp (well-wrung-out) sponge and your choice of cleaners. Examples are mild castile or Ivory soap; a solution of 1/4 cup ammonia to a gallon of water; Murphy's oil soap; and any of a number of good cleaners marketed specifically for leather. Use a minimum amount of water, and scrub off the dirt. A toothbrush may work better than a sponge in some places like the tooling on a western saddle. Choose an appropriate scrubber for the type of leather—in some cases, a soft sponge is best, and in other cases, you can use a table knife (for the underside of western fenders or the wear leathers on the inside of western stirrup leathers) or even steel wool (only for harness leather that is both tough and dirty). Remove the soap with a clean, damp sponge.

While the tack is clean and in pieces, check each piece of leather for wear or broken stitching. Check the buckles for corrosion that may weaken them. Repair at this stage is relatively inexpensive, and you will be safer later.

Your tack may be dry enough to need oiling. Leather dries out (loses its fat content) over a period of time, even with careful use. Horse enthusiasts can tell by the dry feel of the leather that oiling is necessary; ask your instructor to show you how leather feels in different stages of dryness so you can differentiate by feel. By the time you see cracks in the leather, it is too dry and may be permanently damaged.

In between oil applications, some horse enthusiasts use a leather conditioner.

Oil is used to restore the leather's fat content. Neatsfoot oil (compound, or the more expensive pure) is most often used, although there are other oils on the market. The leather should be clean and dry. Apply oil sparingly, and wipe off any excess. Excess oil will come off again, making the leather slippery, collecting dirt, and staining the rider's clothes.

Saddle soap (glycerin-based saddle soap is the one of choice) gives the leather a protective coating. It is used after cleaning and also after oiling the tack. Use a damp sponge and work up a dry lather; rub this lather briskly into the leather. Saddle soap does not need to be rinsed off, but you may need to use a towel to remove the white foam from around the stitching.

Metal parts can be sponged off and wiped dry with a towel. Metal polish may be used on the bit rings and buckles for an extra shine, particularly before a horse show. There is no reason to shine the mouthpiece of the bit, and it may change the taste!

When reassembling stud fasteners on an English bridle, fasten the studs by sliding the end of the leather through both keepers before pressing the stud through the slot in the leather.

English stirrup leathers stretch with use and should be put back on the opposite side of the saddle. This change in position helps keep the leathers even; they stretch unevenly during use because the left one is used in mounting.

The hinged catch on the English stirrup bar is a safety device to free the horse if the stirrup leather or iron gets caught on something and to help free you if you fall with your foot caught in the stirrup. The closed catch cannot be relied upon to open; it usually operates too stiffly. Therefore, leave the safety catch on the stirrup bar down (open) when you put the stirrup leather back on the saddle. The open position of the catch will allow the stirrup leather to slide out to the rear more easily in an emergency.

Cleaning Saddle Pads

The saddle pad must be washed often to remove sweat and dirt. Dried sweat makes the pad stiff, which causes rubbing on the horse's back, and the accumulated salt can be irritating to the skin. The manufacturer may provide cleaning directions. Many pads can be machine washed (much to the chagrin of public laundry-facility managers!—if you use a public facility, clean it thoroughly afterwards) using mild soap. Any soap not rinsed out may irritate the horse's skin, so rinse well. Bleach can be used (with discretion) to restore the color of white pads and to stop the spread of any horse skin infections. An alternative to machine washing is spraying the pad with water and scrubbing it with a brush. If in doubt about your ability to remove all the soap, just use plain water.

Some pads can be machine dried at medium temperatures; others should be line dried. Follow the manufacturer's directions.

Storage Between Rides

Proper storage will keep your tack safely out of the way while making it easily accessible for your next ride. There are lots of opportunities for personal preference in tack storage; a neat and uniform row of saddles and bridles makes the tack room look organized.

The bridle is hung neatly by the crown piece, and the reins must be kept off the ground. Western reins may be draped over the bridle rack. English reins may be hooked through the figure-eight-looped throatlatch (that is held closed by keepers and runners) and the noseband fastened (with the keepers and runners) around everything.

Saddles are best stored on a saddle rack, because this rack maintains their shape. The western cinch may be attached to the off side of the saddle near the horn, or it may hang down. The English stirrup irons are run up the part of the stirrup leather closest to the saddle, and the leathers are put down through the run-up irons. The girth, which is unbuckled at both ends, lies over the seat of the saddle with each end through a stirrup iron. Put the horse's side of the leather girth next to the seat of the saddle to retain its shape.

The unattached pad is draped, wet side up, over the saddle. In addition to letting the pad dry, draping it over the saddle will protect the saddle and keep off dust. If your horse uses additional padding, return this pad to its proper place.

NOTES

12

POSITION OF THE RIDER

A correct, secure, effective position will allow the rider and horse to be comfortable. Horse and rider will move together in balance. The horse will be able to work to its capacity. A good position enables the rider to communicate wishes clearly to the horse in a quiet, effective manner.

There are differences among hunt-, saddle-, stock-, and balance-seat and dressage riding positions, but the principles of balance are similar.

The purpose of this chapter is to reinforce, not replace, your instructor. There are many philosophies regarding riding position. This chapter is meant to clarify the desirable position and explain the reasons for the various components of a correct position.

Security in General

In order to stay balanced as the horse moves, you will make constant, small, instinctive adjustments in your position. It is necessary to ride by balance, not by grip. In fact, stiffening any part of your body will cause tension in the rest of your body and keep you from moving as one with the horse.

The correct leg position is perhaps the most important factor in security.

Stirrup Length

You might begin by adjusting your stirrup length so that the treads hang at or slightly above your ankle bone, tested while you sit centered in the saddle with your legs hanging down. You will eventually be comfortable with the stirrups slightly longer or shorter than this position, depending on the horse's conformation and what you are doing.

A common mistake of novice riders is to ride with the stirrups too long. It is possible to adopt a long stirrup length after learning the correct position, but the length described above facilitates learning to ride with your heels down and calves against the horse. Stirrups adjusted too long cause the rider to straighten and stiffen the legs and possibly point the toes downward; these positions are not compatible with balance and smooth leg aids.

English stirrup length may be estimated from the ground. Hold the stirrup tread in your armpit and stretch your arm straight along the stretched stirrup leather. Your fingers should reach the skirt of the saddle; raise or lower the stirrup depending on your leg-to-arm-length relationship. Test the length after a ride to determine how to set the stirrups for your next ride.

12.1 Correct Position at Halt: Hunt Seat

When using a romal (the quirt that connects the ends of the reins in some western show bridles), the ends of the reins come out of the top of your rein hand, loop around, and join in the romal that is held in your right hand. Hold the romal midway along its length, and lay your right hand on your thigh.

When using split reins, the ends of the reins come out of the bottom part (little finger end) of your hand and hang down on the rein-hand side of the horse's neck. During training, your instructor may have you bridge the reins, crossing them over the neck and holding them in two hands. When using split reins in the show ring, you will not touch the reins with your free hand.

12.2 Correct Position at Halt: Stock Seat

12.3 Correct Position at Halt: Saddle Seat

The Rider's Feet

The feet should be in the stirrups with the widest part (the ball) on the stirrup treads. This position gives stability while allowing flexibility of the ankle. The alternatives are 1) putting just the toes on the stirrup tread, which usually results in losing the stirrup and 2) having the foot in up to the heel (called home), which decreases the up and down range of motion of the ankle and, thus, its flexibility. The "home" position is, however, the most secure in terms of keeping the stirrups and is often the choice of riders encountering rough terrain, particularly at speed.

The pressure you feel on the stirrup tread should be evenly distributed across the stirrup or possibly stronger on the inside of the foot but never stronger on the outside. Correct pressure will help the rider's calves stay against the horse's sides.

The feet should hang naturally, with the toes slightly out. As you sight down your knee, the knee and toe should be forward and out at the same angle to the horse's side. The angle will vary from rider to rider because of differences in rider conformation. Stock-seat riders, particularly, because of the heavy fender of the saddle may find their toes being pulled in while their knees point out slightly. This position causes pain in the knee and outer calf and is solved by molding the fenders and stirrup leathers during storage of the saddle and by stepping down more on the inside of the foot while riding. Forcing the toes to point straight forward (by riders not built this way) stiffens the rider's ankle and rotates the calf away from the horse's sides, preventing sensitive leg use.

Heels Down

When the stirrups are the proper length, the weight of your leg will cause your heel to sink lower than the rest of the foot. This sinking of the heel cannot happen if you grip the saddle with your legs, if you point your toes down, or if your calf muscles lack flexibility. Calf stretching exercises are described in Chapter 14, Rider Exercises on Horseback.

Having weight in your heels is very important for your security. The weight acts as an anchor for the rest of your position, keeping you from being tipped forward if the horse slows suddenly. The more your heel is down (within reason), the longer your effective length of leg is. This leg length gives you security. Having the heel down also stretches out the calf muscle. A stretched, smooth calf is a much more effective aid than the soft calf resulting from the heel being up.

The heels should never be forced down or held down by the rider. Forcing your heels down pushes you away from the saddle, making you top-heavy and insecure. Pushing the heels down can also force your lower legs forward and prevent your being balanced over your legs (you will be off balance to the rear). Riders who push their feet forward and brace against the cantle of a western saddle may feel more secure but will find themselves unable to ride jog and lope as comfortably, will be out of balance when riding uphill, and will not be able to use their legs to signal the horse.

Ankles

The ankles are shock absorbers. They allow the horse to move under you while you keep your feet in the stirrups. You should feel slight horizontal movements of your toes—when sitting a long-strided trot, for example. When you weight your heels (for example, when rising during posting), the ankles should allow your heels to sink. Do not let your ankles bow outward; they cannot support weight in this position and will be limited in their flexibility (they may also hurt).

Calves

Given the correct position of the rest of the leg, your calves should hang close to the horse's sides without muscular effort. They should move softly with the horse's sides. The inside back quarter of your calves should be next to the horse.

As seen from the front, the horse's barrel is egg-shaped in cross section; for most riders on most horses, the barrel is widest below your knee. Your security comes, in part, from having your calves hang down below the widest part of the horse's barrel. This position does not mean that you hold on with your calves, but that you let your legs be long and around the horse rather than up or away from the horse.

Constantly holding on with your calves is incorrect; it is very tiring, keeps you from being able to signal the horse with your calves, and may be interpreted by the horse as a constant signal to speed up.

When you use your legs to signal the horse, squeeze with the part of your calf that is closest to the horse's sides. Depending on the horse's width through the barrel and your leg length, you may use the upper, middle, or lower part of your calf.

Knees

Your knees will not necessarily lie against the saddle; you will probably be able to slide a couple fingers between your knee caps or the inside of your knees and the saddle. This space occurs because of the relative shape of the horse and of your legs. In order to have your calves against the horse, your knees will probably be out somewhat.

It is tiring and ineffective to grip with the knees; gripping with your knee pinches you up out of the saddle and prevents you from attaining a deep seat. Knee grip and lack of calf contact will (at canter, particularly) allow the rider to pivot on the knees, rocking forward and back with the upper body, while the calves pivot in opposite directions. Riders who pinch with their knees may not put enough weight in their stirrups. They will find that their feet keep sliding home in the stirrups or that they lose their stirrups entirely.

Thighs

There will be a certain amount of pressure from your thighs against the saddle. This pressure comes from your weight and from gravity. A common fallacy is that you should hold on with your thighs. While posting to the trot without stirrups, a certain amount of thigh muscle tone is required for intermittent use. However, constant muscle tension will tire you very quickly, make you bounce, and keep you from attaining a good deep seat. The harder you grip with your thighs, the more you will separate your seat from the saddle—just like a simple nutcracker will send the walnut out the open end if you do not lodge it firmly in the nutcracker's teeth and hold on to it with your other hand.

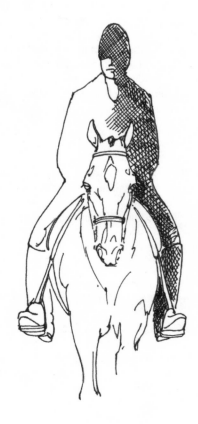

12.4 Front View of Correct Leg Position

Side View of Calves and Feet under Body

See diagrams 12.1 to 12.3 for the correct position at the halt, viewed from the side, for all three seats.

As it is when standing on the ground, you are best balanced when your feet and legs are under you. When seen from the side, your foot should be under or slightly ahead of a vertical line that drops down from your shoulder and bisects your hip. Your stirrup leather/fender will hang vertically, and a small portion of the girth/cinch will be visible in front of your foot.

Your feet are too far in front of you if you can see your toes in front of your knees as you sit in the saddle. Another good way to find out if your feet and calves are properly under you is to rise into two-point position (see Chapter 13, Two-Point Position). If you can stay up in two-point position, your calves and feet are under your body. If you find yourself sitting down, it is because your feet are too far out in front of your body. If you tip forward in two-point position, it is because your calves and feet are too far back or your heels are up.

The Seat

You should feel your seat bones (the lowest protrusions of your pelvis) against the saddle. It is incorrect to rock back on your tail bone or to sit forward on your crotch. Generally, the correct riding position should not hurt (if you have sore muscles, stretching before riding and periodically during your ride will help). If you are taking a long ride, sitting correctly on your seat bones before you become accustomed to this position can hurt; ride in two-point position occasionally to relieve the pressure.

You should sit in the lowest part of the saddle (assuming the saddle has been built correctly and sits correctly on the horse's back). Do not be tempted to brace your feet forward and sit back against the cantle; besides taking constant muscle effort to maintain, this position puts your weight farther back than the saddle is designed for and may make the horse's back sore.

Riding in the lowest part of the saddle and letting gravity keep you there is part of the "deep seat" riders strive for. This position involves controlled relaxation that allows gravity to keep your seat in the saddle with a minimum of energy expended.

Hips

Hip angle. As viewed from the side, the angle between the upper body and thigh is the hip angle. The hip angle closes (decreases) and opens (increases) in response to the horse's balance, when signaling the horse, and during rider exercises or practice. At halt, walk, sitting trot, jog, and lope, the hip angle is mostly open and does not vary much. It opens and closes some for canter, more for posting, and is more closed during two-point position.

If you are supple enough, you will find your hips constantly moving as you ride. Not only will your pelvis rock forward and back, but your hips will sway very slightly from side to side. At first, you may need to make a conscious effort to follow with your hips, but your goal is a relaxed following motion as the horse moves under you.

Lateral hip flexibility. The correct leg position is easier to obtain if there is some lateral flexibility in the hip joints, in addition to the above-mentioned longitudinal flexibility. Lateral flexibility allows you to stretch your legs wide to sit on wide-barreled horses. As with the other position criteria, there are exercises that can be done, both on and off the horse, to increase lateral flexibility in the hip joints.

Upper Body

In order to be able to follow the horse's motion with your hips, you need to be flexible in your waist. This flexibility is facilitated by stretching your upper body tall and feeling your rib cage being suspended above your pelvis, not resting on it. Seen from the side, your lower back should not be swayed (very concave) or rounded.

Correct posture requires concentration until it becomes a habit. Practice good posture during the times you are not riding. Sitting elegantly will be easier to do when you ride if that is the way you sit when you are not riding.

Your upper body should stretch up until your shoulders are back. Getting the shoulders back is not achieved by pulling them there; force causes tension. Instead, take a deep breath that raises your chest, and stretch your upper body upward. Some riders feel this position as the collar bones being forward. In this position, you will find that the shoulders' natural position is down and back and that your shoulder blades are correctly flat against your back.

Your elbows will hang near your sides, and when viewed from the side, the elbow(s) of your rein hand(s) may be beside or slightly in front of your body.

In general across all riding styles, there will be a straight line between the rider's elbow and the bit (the forearm and rein are along this line, particularly when the rider has contact with the horse's mouth). This alignment means that saddle-seat riders with higher-headed horses will ride with their hands higher than those on western saddles whose horses carry their heads lower.

Wrists

The wrist(s) should be straight, not arching up or breaking down and not twisting to hold the hands horizontal or vertical. Straight wrists are the most supple and will allow the most sensitive communication with your horse's mouth. Your wrists should be in a state of controlled relaxation, which is how you want the horse's mouth to feel.

Hands

English snaffle reins are held so that they come from the horse's mouth, run outside your little finger or between your little and ring fingers, and into your closed hands. The end (bight) of the reins comes out from between the first finger and thumb and hangs forward along the horse's shoulder inside the rest of the rein. The thumb holds the rein(s) flat against the second knuckle of the first finger.

Curb reins, alone, may be held together as described above, with the little finger separating them. Or the reins can come from the bit, in between the thumb and first finger (or with the first finger separating them), and out below the little finger.

Double reins are held with the curb on top of the snaffle; they come into the lower part of the hand with the little finger separating the two reins and come out the top of the hand as single snaffle reins do.

The hand(s) are closed without being clenched. They are closed to prevent dropping the reins but not clenched, because clenching the reins causes unnecessary tension. Do not confuse educated, sensitive hands with incorrectly open fingers.

The rein hand(s) should be over and above the withers, with the knuckles approximately 30 degrees inside the vertical. Flat (horizontal) hands, like arched or broken (angled) wrists, interfere with sensitive communication.

The hand(s) must stay as steady as possible to facilitate quiet aids and to avoid giving unintentional signals. With practice, your rein hand(s) will become independent of your body movements. When your body position is correct and you stay balanced at all times, you will be able to give subtle and much clearer rein signals. You will begin to develop educated hands. Until then, do not expect to ride with contact on your horse's mouth (as you will do later if you are riding with a snaffle).

Shortening the Reins

When shortening the reins an inch or two, crawl up them (toward the horse's mouth) with your fingers. Keep your fingers closed as much as possible. If the horse should stumble or toss its head while you are changing your hand position, you will not drop the reins. This method of shortening the reins is the only correct way when riding western with a curb bit in a horse show; you are not allowed to touch the reins with your free hand (riding with a romal is an exception).

When riding with two hands on the reins (with a snaffle bit) and when the reins must be shortened more than a couple inches, one hand is used at a time to adjust the opposite rein. Keeping the left hand softly closed, use the right hand to pull the left rein through until the rein is the correct length. Then use the left hand to shorten the right rein.

Head and Eyes

As you stretch upward into the correct upper body position, continue upward with your head. Your balance and control will be best when your eyes and head are up. Look out ahead of you, and let your glance include other parts of the arena or both sides of the trail, as well. Avoid the impulse to look at the ground or at your horse's neck. Looking down rounds your shoulders and changes your balance. If you have to look down, do so with your eyes, but leave your chin up.

Concentration

Perfecting your riding requires concentration. You may find that you would like to be able to concentrate better and for longer periods of time. Your ability to concentrate can be improved if you work to do so. However, there will be times when outside thoughts get in the way. Do not get frustrated; it might just be a good day for a relaxing hack through the woods!

Details

Practicing riding skills requires attention to many details at the same time. Your ability to get everything correct at the same time will improve as you ride. If you get frustrated, try to concentrate on one thing at a time. There is often one position weakness or one detail that, when correct, will make a big improvement in your riding. Have your instructor help you concentrate on the most important (at the moment) thing to work on. Whatever you are working on, do it as well as you possibly can. Remember that practice alone does not make perfect; perfect practice makes perfect.

Feedback

All levels of riders need someone on the ground to help them. Beginners and intermediates need feedback to progress, and more advanced riders will benefit from feedback on how the horse is moving. Without the knowledge of the whole horse-and-rider picture from the ground, it is easy to develop bad habits (especially in position) and to accept an incorrect carriage or movement by the horse.

Photographs are good for position analysis, but it takes a skilled photographer and good interpretation to get the most out of them. Videotapes are excellent. They allow you a continuous picture of yourself that can be slowed and paused for analysis and repeated at will. Review the photographs or tapes while the feeling of your ride is fresh in your mind, and go over them with your instructor or ground person.

Different Philosophies of Riding

While describing rider position, which will vary according to instructor interpretation and philosophy, it is appropriate to mention riding philosophies.

Different instructors have different philosophies of riding. There are also many different methods of teaching. Find an instructor you trust whose philosophies agree with yours and with whom you are comfortable, and do not hesitate to ask questions at appropriate times.

Input from different instructors will enhance your understanding; there may be differences in their explanations that suddenly make concepts clear to you. Some information gained from the second instructor may be confusing in light of your experience to date. Ask questions, and rather than trying to determine who is wrong or right (perhaps both are correct!), use what seems best for you at the time, and store the rest away for future reference.

NOTES

13

TWO-POINT POSITION

Known as two-point, galloping, or jumping position or floating, this position moves the weight that was in the rider's seat to the thighs and stirrups. It allows the seat to float above the saddle, freeing the horse's back during galloping and jumping. It is also an extremely useful exercise to establish and strengthen the leg position for hunt- and stock-seat riders.

When you rise out of the saddle into two-point position, you do not merely stand up in your stirrups. Standing in the stirrups does not allow you to stay in balance on a moving horse. Instead of standing, keep your ankle, knee, and hip angles closed, your feet under you, your back stretched tall with a slight arch in your lower back, and your eyes up. Staying flexible through your whole body will allow your balance to adapt to any move the horse may make.

Correctly ridden, two-point position puts your weight on your inner thighs, calves, stirrups, and heels. Your knees should be as low as possible (not pinched and raised). Your calves will hug the horse's sides. This position gives you the lowest possible center of gravity (knees and heels down), maximum shock absorption (in flexed knees and ankles), a way to keep close to the saddle (calves low around the horse's sides), and the ability to keep your weight off the horse's back.

13.1 Two-Point Position

77

Feet and Lower Legs

The key to security is a correct leg and foot position. Your feet should be under you for maximum balance. If you allow your lower legs to slip out in front of you, you will find yourself sinking back into the saddle. If your lower legs are too far back, you will feel yourself tipping forward.

Your calves will help you balance if you let them lie against your horse's sides. As when you are sitting, the inside back quarter of your calf should touch the horse lightly.

You might need to open your knees—take them away from the saddle—a little to allow your calves to come in. Let your toes be out according to the way you are built. When you lean forward and sight down your knees, you should see your toes pointing forward and out at the same angle as your knees. Most riders are correct when their toes point out a bit. Your ankles should not bend out; they may stay straight or flex in slightly. This position will give you the feeling that the weight on your feet is evenly distributed on or perhaps slightly to the inside of the stirrup treads. Be certain you have enough of each foot in the stirrup to keep the stirrup but not so much that your heels cannot go down. The balls of your feet (the wide part behind your toes) work well for maintaining this position.

Your ankles, viewed from the side, should be bent. Your heels will be lower than your toes, even more so than when you were sitting, because the weight previously supported by your seat is now going down through your knees and past the stirrup into your heels. If you keep your ankles flexible, you will feel your knees slide down on the saddle flap/fender and your heels sink as you rise into two-point position and with each step or stride of the horse. The knees sliding down and forward lower your center of gravity and make you more secure; gripping is not required. When the knees and ankles stay bent and are flexible, two-point position will allow your body to be smoothly carried above the horse. The shock of the horse's movement at trot, canter, jump, and riding cross-country will be comfortably taken up by these supple joints.

Hip Angle

Your hip angle (the angle between your upper body and thigh as viewed from the side) is more closed than it was when you were sitting. It will be more closed in hunt- than stock-seat riding. The more closed your hip angle, the closer your chest will be to the horse's neck. Be certain to breathe deeply so you do not collapse your chest. Putting a slight arch in your lower back (letting your belt buckle come forward) will help you incline your upper body forward correctly from the hips instead of incorrectly bending at the waist. When seen from the side, it will be obvious that having your buttocks behind you balances your chest and shoulders, which are in front. Your body must balance over your lower legs. The same flexibility that is required in your ankles and knees is needed in your hips in order to stay in dynamic balance with the horse.

Eyes

Continue to look up so you can see where you are going. Looking down does not only invite accidents; it upsets your balance, as well.

Hands

Shorten your reins. Shortened reins are necessary, because your upper body is more forward and closer to the horse's neck than it is sitting and posting positions; your arms are also more forward. You will want to keep the same amount of slack in your reins as you had sitting or posting, so it is necessary to shorten your reins.

When riding in a hunt-seat saddle, learning two-point position can be facilitated by balancing your hands (usually the second bone of your fingers) lightly on the horse's neck. Move your hands forward (about six inches or about one-third of the way up the horse's neck) to rest on the animal's neck. Too far a reach will unbalance you, as will leaving your hands too far back. Rest your knuckles on either side of or close to the crest of the horse's neck. You can hold a handful of mane with the rein in one hand to keep from pulling the horse in the mouth if you should sit down accidentally. When riding western style, you can use the horn—use a couple fingers around the front of it. If you tip forward, you can push yourself back up with your hands. You may take one hand off the neck to steer. As your balance improves, you will be able to ride in two-point position at all gaits without needing to balance with your hand(s).

When your two-point position is stabilized on the flat, you will be ready to ride over cavalletti and, in a hunt-seat saddle, begin to jump.

14

RIDER EXERCISES ON HORSEBACK

Riding is an athletic activity and should be approached as any such activity: warm-up and strength-building exercises are integral parts. Some warm-up activities are best done on the ground before mounting; other exercises are done on the horse. Performing exercises on horseback will help the rider warm up for riding, relax mentally and physically, develop balance, increase suppleness, improve coordination, improve timing, and build strength. The resulting more secure seat will give the rider more independent hands and improve communication with the horse.

The exercises here are some of the many useful ones available. This list of exercises and their descriptions will help the rider understand the value of the exercises the individual is asked to do in classes. As the rider progresses, the individual takes the initiative to plan a personal warm-up; this list can be used to find appropriate personal exercises.

The exercises listed below are generally accepted as being useful for riders. However, each rider has the responsibility of choosing exercises that are compatible with the individual's physical situation and any medical conditions.

Some exercises are of particular use when done at certain gaits, at sitting trot/jog versus rising trot, in two-point position, with or without stirrups, or while jumping a series of fences. The horse must be in control during exercises; the horse can be held by someone on the ground, it may be on a longe line, or riders with the ability may control the horse themselves. It is the rider's and instructor's responsibility to choose appropriate exercises and to carry them out safely.

When the rider is doing exercises without stirrups, the English stirrup irons may be left hanging or the stirrup leathers may be crossed. Crossing the leathers is traditionally done by crossing the left leather over the right across the horse's neck after pulling each buckle down six inches. Pulling the buckle down gets it out of the way and allows the leathers to be flattened under the skirt so they do not form a bulge under the rider's thigh. Having the left leather on top makes it easy to bring it down for dismounting or mounting.

Many of the listed activities are stretching exercises. The maximum benefit will be realized when the rider concentrates on stretching slowly, as far as possible in each direction.

Exercises Related to the Parts of the Body

BODY PART AFFECTED	RELATED EXERCISE
1. Neck	a. Neck stretches
2. Shoulders	a. Shoulder rolls b. Arm circles c. Elbow circles

3. Upper Body	a. Arms
	     1. up
	     2. out to sides
	     3. twist to rear (trunk twists)
	b. Hands
	     1. on head
	     2. on back of neck
	     3. on shoulder
	     4. on hips
	     5. on thighs

BODY PART AFFECTED	RELATED EXERCISE

3. Upper Body	b. Hands
	     6. touch part of horse
	        named by instructor
	     7. hang at sides
	c. Hands behind
	     1. upper back
	     2. lower back
	d. Cheerleader
	e. Rope climbing

4. Back	a. Hat brim to croup

5. Hip Angle	a. Lie on
	     1. neck
	     2. croup
	b. Crest release

6. Hips, laterally	a. Frog b. Thighs away c. Straight-legged hip stretch (scissors)
7. Thighs	a. Thigh muscle out behind leg b. Calves up
8. Knees	a. Calf swings

9. Calves	a. Hold stirrup
	     leathers/fenders against
	     girth/cinch

10. Ankles	a. Ankle circles b. Toes in and out
11. Legs	a. Two-point position b. Toe-heel stretch c. Toe touches d. Ride without stirrups e. Post without stirrups

Exercise Descriptions

1a. Neck stretches. Tilt head forward, and then up; to one side, and then up. Feel the neck muscles stretching. This stretching exercise is particularly good for relieving tension in the neck and shoulders.

2a. Shoulder rolls. Bring one or both shoulders up, back, and down in a smooth, continuous motion. The opposite motion, forward rolls, has limited usefulness, because it encourages rounded shoulders. This exercise can help riders who hunch their shoulders.

2b. Arm circles. Straightened arms revolve to the rear in a slow sweeping motion. The whole upper body is loosened if the rider rotates one arm and watches that hand.

2c. Elbow circles. With fingers on shoulders, the rider circles the elbows to the rear. This exercise is a variation of arm circles.

3a1. Arms up. The rider may slump with the upper body first and then rise slowly while inhaling until the arms reach upward as far as possible. The exercise ends by the rider retaining the tall position after lowering the arms. This exercise helps open (widen) the chest, straighten the back, and loosen the lower back.

3a2. Arms out to sides. One or both arms is/are held straight out at shoulder height. Holding the palms up makes this exercise helpful in opening the chest.

3a3. Arms twist to rear (trunk twists). The rider holds the arms out, palms up, as in exercise 3a2. The individual alternately twists slowly to one side and then to the other side with the whole upper body. Watching the rearward hand will help with suppling and will improve the rider's balance.

3b1–7. Hands on head, back of neck, shoulders, hips, thighs, named part of horse, or hang at sides. These exercises improve balance. They give the rider something to concentrate on, so the individual lets instinctive balance take over. Hands on shoulders or on back of neck with elbows held wide helps open the chest. Hands on hips helps the rider feel when the individual is following the horse's movement with the hips. Touching the parts of the horse named by the instructor reviews the student's knowledge of the parts of the horse.

Letting one hand hang at the side and the other hand hold the reins is an excellent correction for a rider who normally rides two-handed and does too much with the reins or balances on them.

3c1. Hands behind upper back. Either the elbow is up while the palm is held between the shoulder blades or the elbow is down while the back of the hand reaches between the shoulder blades. One elbow can be up while the other is down, and the rider touches the fingers together if both hands are free. This exercise pulls the shoulders back and opens the chest.

3c2. Hands behind lower back. One or both hands are held behind the lower back. This exercise is useful for showing a rider how to close the hip angle instead of bending at the waist, particularly over fences.

3d. Cheerleader. Done continuously at canter on the longe line, this exercise helps the rider stop pumping with the upper body. On four successive strides, both hands swing down, above head, down, and to chest.

3e. Rope climbing. Performed as exercise 3d, Cheerleader, this activity is another balance and upper-body suppling exercise. The rider imitates climbing a rope with the hands while cantering on a longe line.

4a. Hat brim to croup. The rider turns around, faces the tail, places both hands on the croup, and stretches to touch the individual's hat brim to the croup. This exercise is a good way to stretch the back. Performed at walk or halt, this exercise is best done with a ground person handling the horse.

5a1. Lie on neck. Without letting the calves swing backward, the rider lies on the horse's neck (for English riders only!). The stretch is felt in the back and in the backs of the thighs.

5a2. Lie on croup. The front of the thighs are stretched and the hip angle is opened by this exercise. The lower legs must stay in place on the girth/cinch. The reins are not to be used to balance or to help the rider sit up. This exercise is best done with a horse handler on the ground.

5b. Crest release. From two-point position, close the hip angle a few degrees and move the hands forward, placing the knuckles on the crest. The rider must be certain not to bend at the waist instead of the hip, so the student should remember to keep the back straight. This exercise is good practice before jumping, because it mimics the motion of jumping. When jumping, the horse's action causes the rider's hip angle to close.

6a. Frog. Both legs, bent at the knee, are raised off the saddle until the feet are suspended over the horse's shoulders. Hold this position as long as possible. Avoid leaning back. The pommel/horn may be held for support. This exercise opens the hips laterally, and stretching in the hip joint ligaments will be felt if it is done correctly.

6b. Thighs away. Both thighs are lifted directly sideways off the saddle. When done correctly, stretching will be felt in the hip joint ligaments. This activity is an excellent exercise to increase the lateral flexibility of the hips and to let the rider know what it feels like to not hold on with the knees.

6c. Straight-legged hip stretch (scissors). This exercise helps to increase the range of motion of the hip joints. It helps the rider move the outside leg back to signal the horse. With the knee straight, the rider stretches one leg forward and the other back. When done correctly, the rider will feel stretching in the hip joint ligaments.

7a. Thigh muscle out behind leg. Especially helpful for the rider with heavy thighs, this exercise correctly places the flat inside of the thigh against the saddle. Whenever the rider feels the heavy back part of the thigh getting in the way under the leg, the individual opens the knees, brings the leg to the rear, and then slides it forward into place. This position leaves the heavy part of the thigh out behind the leg. The rider may also pull the rear part of the thigh out by hand.

7b. Calves up. The rider brings both calves to horizontal position (or as close as possible) by bending the knees. Then the rider stretches the knees down until the hips and front thigh muscles stretch. The student does not grip the horse's sides with the knees, calves, or heels. This exercise helps the rider get the legs down and around a wide horse.

8a. Calf swings. The knees are stationary while the calves swing forward and back. This exercise relaxes the legs and is particularly useful after any riding that may tense the legs.

9a. Hold stirrup leathers/fenders against girth/cinch. Used while riding at trot/jog or canter/lope without stirrups, this exercise helps the rider feel the calves correctly against the horse's sides at the back edge of the girth/cinch. Useful for riders whose calves slide back or who hold on with their knees.

10a. Ankle circles. Making wide circles with the toes in both directions relaxes the ankles.

10b. Toes in and out. Done with stirrups at sitting trot/jog and canter/lope, this exercise helps the rider feel the suppleness in the ankles that is necessary for rhythmic use of the leg aids. The toes are turned in and out on a horizontal plane in rhythm with the horse's strides.

11a. Two-point position. Discussed in detail in Chapter 13, Two-Point Position, this position is an excellent exercise to balance a rider over the legs, to get the weight down into the heels, and to strengthen the legs.

11b. Toe-heel stretch. From two-point position, the rider rises onto the toes, straightens the knees, and opens the hip angle. The student may hold the mane/horn. Then the rider sinks back down to two-point position (not to a sitting position). One angle at a time (ankles, knees, or hips) may be flexed to increase awareness of the hip angle and of the sinking down of the knees and heels. The toes must remain slightly out, pointing in the same direction as the knees. The knees should slip down on the saddle leather (versus being held tight to the saddle) when the rider is sinking down.

11c. Toe touches. Without allowing the other lower leg to swing back, the rider touches a toe with the same or opposite hand. The stretch will be felt in the back and in the back of the thigh and calf.

11d. Ride without stirrups. A common test at equitation competitions, this exercise shows the extent of the rider's balance and security. The rider should work until the individual rides as well without stirrups as with them. The leg position should mimic the one with stirrups, including the heels being down.

11e. Post without stirrups. This exercise strengthens the legs.

THE AIDS AND THEIR USE

The aids are our signals that communicate to the horse what we want the animal to do. We use these aids in ever-changing series and combinations to shape the horse's body and movements.

The horse does not automatically associate the signals with what we want it to do. We must apply the aid best suited to the response, wait and watch for the desired response, and reward (mostly by releasing the pressure) the horse's slightest try. After we consistently get the desired response, we can increase the complexity of the aids. Taking the horse through progressive steps, we increase the complexity of the aids and the expected results until the horse is executing complex maneuvers.

Aids are not a one-way communication system; we must feel, see, and sense the horse's responses and adapt our signals based on what the horse is offering.

To a horse that does not understand, stronger signals are not helpful; response to aids is a trained behavior. For example, if a rider exceeds the horse's pain threshold by abusive use of the bit or spurs, the horse will behave out of fear or instinct rather than by a trained response.

The aids are applied in a squeeze-and-release or tapping motion. The horse cannot be forced to respond, so there is no use in stiffening your body and pulling or pushing for an extended time.

You must insist on getting the correct response to each signal. Otherwise you are undoing the horse's training; you are teaching the horse that it does not have to respond that way to that aid; you are making the animal less responsive. For that reason, continue to hold, vibrate, or tap with the aid until the horse responds. If the horse does not respond, check your signal to be sure it is correct. Then intensify the aid or back it up with a stronger one.

Once the horse responds, cease the aid. Ceasing the aid is the horse's reward for performing correctly. As your feeling and timing improve, you can stop asking when the horse begins to respond; this process is the path to the ideal subtleness of communication between rider and horse. Keep the aids ready to use again.

Riders strive to communicate with the lightest possible aids. In order to do this, you should always ask with the lightest possible aid and increase it only as you need to. Even if you needed to be very strong last time, go back to using a light aid. Chances are the horse will remember the succession to stronger aids and respond to the lighter one.

The horse will work best if many subtle signals are used to communicate your wishes to the animal. The appearance of an effortless ride is the result of your constant attention to and continuous communication with the horse. You are constantly shaping the horse and its movements into your ideal mental picture (which is actually more like a videotape!) of the horse.

Although this is a simplification, for basic understanding we can group the aids into two general categories: natural and artificial.

Natural Aids

Natural aids are those directly from your body. Legs, hands, weight or seat, and voice are your natural aids. The first three take advantage of the horse's sensitivity to pressure; riding puts us in a good position to influence the horse with these aids. The fourth aid is less often used but is very effective because of the horse's acute hearing.

Legs. The leg aids are primarily used to ask the horse to go forward. They also establish and keep bend. Their influence on the hindquarters allows the rider to signal for turns and move the hindquarters sideways as well. Experienced riders also use their legs, coordinated with their hands, to collect the horse.

The inside back quarter of your calf is used in a squeeze-and-release motion on the horse's side(s). If the desired response does not occur or comes too slowly, intensify the aid. Horses that have been ridden in lesson programs learn to tune out subtle leg signals, because they get conflicting, unclear, and unrewarded signals from riders who are busy finding their own balance and coordination. It may be necessary to kick once, sharply, to get the horse's attention and then go back to leg squeezes as aids.

The whole length of your calf will probably not touch the horse. Use the part that naturally hangs closest to the horse's side. Do not raise your heel to use it; raising your heel pulls your leg up, out of position.

The legs can be used in the position called "at the girth/cinch," which is where the leg normally hangs at the rear edge of the girth/cinch. Either leg can also be used behind the girth/cinch. In this position, the leg is stretched backward, both from the hip and by bending the knee slightly, and used four to six inches behind where it normally lies. The heel is not raised, nor is the calf brought up toward a horizontal position when the leg is stretched back.

Your legs can be used rhythmically to dictate the rhythm and tempo of the gait. At walk, the legs contact the horse's sides alternately. At trot, the legs are used together. In canter, the outside leg comes into contact with the horse's side slightly before the inside one during each stride.

Hands. The hands influence the front of the horse. Through the reins, which are extensions of your hands, you can stop or slow the horse, turn the animal, and have it rebalance more of its weight from its forehand to its hindquarters.

Hand signals are felt by the horse through the reins on the horse's neck, head, and mouth. You squeeze and release with your fingers (if you are riding with a feel of the horse's mouth) and move your hands to signal the horse. The release comes only after (but just as soon as) you feel a response from the horse.

Weight. Your weight can be a subtle aid or a strong one, depending on how it is used. Weight can also be used carelessly (as the other aids can be) and may cause unwanted reactions. Used most often in conjunction with other aids, it can speed up, slow down, or turn the horse. Sometimes called the seat for the part of your body the horse feels when you change your weight, this aid becomes more useful as you learn to control your movement in the saddle.

Slight movement of your upper body forward encourages the horse to move forward. Movement of your shoulders back to a vertical position tells the horse to gather itself, to slow down, or to stop.

Voice. The voice works as an aid only because of normal association with other correctly applied aids. It must not—cannot—replace the other natural aids. It should be used sparingly if you will be riding with others, as the horses will listen to other riders. Look to your instructor for appropriate voice aids for the horses you will be riding. This section will also be helpful in understanding the use of the voice when you are working around the horse on the ground, in the round pen, or on the longe line.

The horse reacts to the tone of your voice rather than interpreting the words you use. Therefore, pay attention to the tone and be consistent in it when you expect the same response. For example, to calm a tense horse or slow one that is rushing, the soothing tone of voice is more important than the words you choose.

Examples of common voice commands and their use include a firm "whoa," usually pronounced "ho," for signaling the horse to halt. Use it only when you are making the horse halt, not when you want to slow down. Otherwise the aid will begin to mean "slow down." (Your instructor may use another command for slowing down.) A click of the tongue can be used to tell the horse to move out faster. Generally this sound is used as you would other aids: in the rhythm you want the horse to travel.

Artificial Aids

Artificial aids are those communication helpers that you carry or wear or that the horse wears as additional equipment.

The most common artificial aid is carried by the rider. It is called a crop, whip, quirt, stick, or bat, depending on its shape. The term crop will be used here to mean all such aids. Experienced riders may wear spurs as an artificial aid. The two most common artificial aids worn by the horse are running and standing martingales.

Crop. The crop is carried when it is needed to get the horse's attention and to reinforce the horse's response to the leg aids. If the reins are carried in both hands, the crop may be held with either rein. If the reins are held together, the crop is held in the free hand. The leather flap or piece of cord (the business end) points down and back, toward your thigh. If it is long enough, it will rest across your thigh at an angle. The crop may be switched from hand to hand depending on how the horse is acting. If the horse is not listening to your outside leg when you tell the animal to canter/lope, for example, carry the crop in your outside hand. This way you can reinforce your outside leg aid. If the horse is not listening to your inside leg and comes in toward the center, carry the crop on the inside. There are a number of techniques of moving the crop across from one hand to the other; ask your instructor for the preferred technique. The important thing is not to wave the crop around and make the horse wonder if you are about to use it, but to keep it close to your body and the horse's body and switch it smoothly from one side to the other while keeping control of the reins.

Some crops come with a strap to wear around your wrist. For beginners, it is safer not to use this strap; there may be a time when you want to drop the crop without losing control of the reins. Experienced riders riding cross-country sometimes do use a strap or rubber band that will break in case of a fall; this strap will help keep them from dropping and losing the crop.

When you give the horse a clear, strong, correct leg aid and the animal does not respond, use the crop immediately to reinforce the leg aid. Do not merely hit the horse with the crop as an initial aid; the animal will not learn to respond to your legs this way.

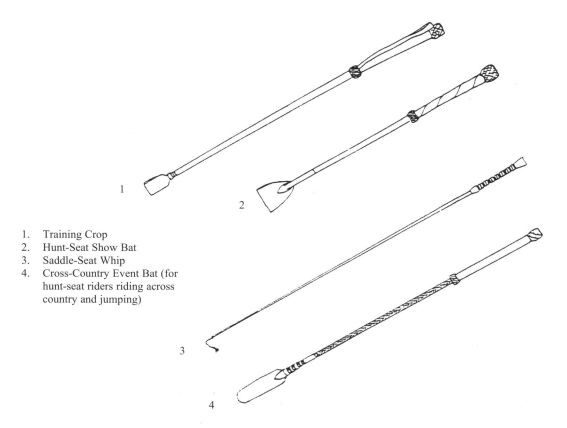

1. Training Crop
2. Hunt-Seat Show Bat
3. Saddle-Seat Whip
4. Cross-Country Event Bat (for hunt-seat riders riding across country and jumping)

15.1 Bat, Crop, and Whip

85

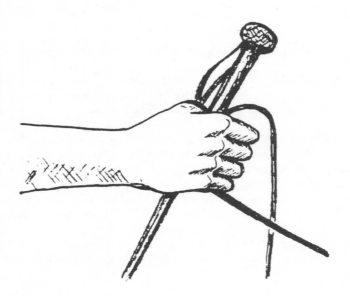

To use the crop, put/keep both reins in one hand. Riders who cannot guarantee the stability of this rein hand should rest that hand on the crest of the horse's neck with a little slack in the reins. This position ensures that you keep the rein hand steady while you use the crop. Otherwise, as the horse responds to the aid and moves forward, you may momentarily lose your balance backward and catch the horse in the mouth. This clashing of aids (telling the horse to go forward with the crop and telling it to slow down with your accidental hand movement) is very confusing to the horse. (Experienced riders with long dressage whips will be able to use the whip with the rein remaining in the hand and not clash the aids.) Use the crop to hit the horse once, hard, right behind your leg. The crop reinforces your leg aid, so it makes sense to use it in as close to where you used your leg as possible. The crop aid is more effective if it is used once, hard, than if it intermittently taps at the horse. This aid is not meant to hurt the horse; it works because it makes a sharp sound when it hits the animal. Continue riding as before, and feel that the horse now responds to your leg aids because the horse wants to avoid the consequences of not responding.

Spurs. Spurs are an effective artificial aid when used by experienced riders. The rider must be able to feel what the legs are doing at all times and control the leg position to avoid accidentally spurring the horse. Riders without this control should not wear spurs. Spurs, properly used in sequence, heighten the sensitivity of the horse to the leg aids; the horse learns to respond to a light leg aid to avoid the spur that follows when the animal does not respond. One or both spurs are used immediately after the leg aid any time the horse does not respond to the leg. The rider then returns to using the legs alone and saves the spur for reinforcement.

Martingales. Martingales are artificial aids worn by the horse. The standing martingale (English) or tie-down (western) and running martingale influence the horse's head position. One advantage of these two artificial aids is their consistency. They are always there to signal the horse when the animal raises its head to a certain height.

Standing martingale and tie down. These aids work basically the same; the former is the English term, the latter is the western one. One end of the standing martingale attaches to the girth between the horse's front legs; the other end attaches to the noseband of the bridle. A strap around the base of the horse's neck keeps the martingale from hanging low enough to cause an accident. The tie down consists of a strap from the cinch or breast plate and a special nosepiece that is added to the western bridle for this purpose.

Both aids keep the horse from raising its head too high; when the horse does, it feels pressure on its nose.

The common standing-martingale adjustment is made while the horse is standing with its head in a normal position. The martingale strap is pushed up and should just touch the horse's throat (see diagram 15.4).

15.3 Using the Crop

15.4 Standing Martingale

Running martingale. One end of the running martingale attaches to the girth/cinch between the horse's front legs or to the western breast plate. The other end is split, with rings on the ends of the two straps. The reins go through these rings. A neck strap keeps the English running martingale up near the chest. The running martingale does not influence the horse as long as the reins are loose. If the rider takes up on the reins and feels the horse's mouth and if the horse carries its head higher than it should, the martingale rings change the angle of the rein pressure on the horse's mouth. The downward angle of the reins created by the martingale rings mimics the angle when the horse's head is carried at an appropriate height but is too far forward. The rings allow the rider to keep the hands in the same place and influence the horse even when the horse tries to evade the direction and pressure by raising its head. When the horse consistently feels pressure when it raises its head, the horse seeks the relief it gets when it lowers its head; the horse learns to carry its head at the appropriate height and is reminded to flex at the poll.

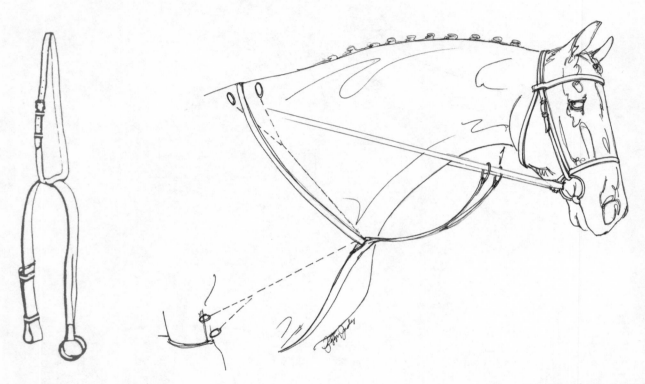

15.5 Running Martingale

The running martingale is used with snaffle bits as opposed to curbs in lesson horses; the combination of curb and martingale is a powerful aid to lowering the horse's head and is best left to educated hands.

The running-martingale adjustment varies from situation to situation. There are three common ways to check the length of the ring straps: while the horse is standing normally, while the neck strap is fastened, and while the rings are free of the reins. The rings should reach either 1) the horse's throat, 2) the horse's elbow, or 3) the crest of the neck where the neck strap crosses it. See diagram 15.5.

Either of the two types of martingales described above can be effective training tools that are discarded when no longer necessary. If the situation dictates, however, they may be used on a long-term basis. Standing martingales, for example, are allowed in hunter classes over fences at horse shows.

REIN AIDS

The various movement-shaping and position-influencing ways to use the reins are often classified to facilitate communication (between humans!). One common way is to identify the aids as one of five methods: direct, indirect in front of the withers, indirect behind the withers, bearing or neck rein, and opening or leading rein. Additionally, the pulley rein is reserved for emergency use with snaffle bridles, and the one-rein stop is both a training and working maneuver.

The beginning rider rides with slack in the reins to avoid unnecessary motion on the horse's mouth as the rider finds balance. When giving rein aids (except for some uses of neck rein), the slack must first be gently taken out of the reins to avoid jerking the horse in the mouth. As the rider advances and is able to keep the hands independent of the body, the individual is able to ride with shorter reins (with a curb) or a feel of the horse's mouth (snaffle). These techniques make more delicate rein aids possible.

Direct Rein

Any slack must first gently be taken out of the rein(s). The aiding hand or hands move(s) straight back, putting direct (as opposed to sideways) pressure on the horse's mouth. There is a straight line from the bit, through the hand, and to the elbow when viewed from the side. When seen from above, the rider using two hands will bring the elbows back, preserving the straight line from bit to each elbow. The rider using one hand (western) will bring that hand back toward the body.

One direct snaffle rein will cause a turn in that direction; both direct snaffle or curb reins will slow down, collect, or stop the horse.

When riding on contact and using a direct rein to turn, the other rein may be used to influence the amount of bend in the horse's neck and to increase or to decrease the radius of the turn.

16.1 Direct Rein

Indirect Rein in Front of the Withers

Snaffle. One hand pivots from its usual 30-degree angle inside the vertical to 30 degrees outside the vertical while the wrist stays supple. This pivot brings the little finger closer to the rider's body. Pressure of varying degrees may be applied; this pressure (and the line, as seen from above in diagram 16.2) is from the bit ring on the hand side toward the rider's opposite hip.

Curb. The rein hand is carried across the neck (for example, to the right side), putting light pressure back and to the right. Done during a turn to the left, this aid is a left indirect rein aid (see diagram 16.2).

This rein aid positions the horse's head to that side. A common use is to position the horse correctly looking into a turn. Because of its indirect action, it influences the horse 1) not to turn too soon or too sharply and 2) to avoid leaning to the inside of the turn. This rein aid acts to shift the horse's weight toward its opposite (outside) foreleg.

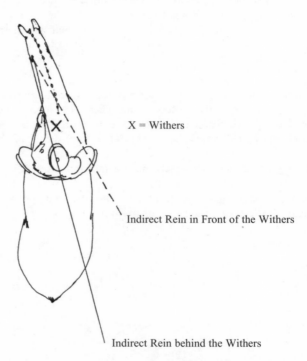

X = Withers

Indirect Rein in Front of the Withers

Indirect Rein behind the Withers

16.2 Indirect Rein in Front of and behind the Withers

Indirect Rein behind the Withers

This aid is similar to the indirect rein in front except that the hand and arm exert more backward pressure on the horse's mouth. The pressure is in a line from the bit (on the hand side—English; on the side where the hand is carried—western) toward the horse's opposite hip. This line falls behind the withers, hence its name.

This rein aid also positions the horse's head toward the hand's side and shifts the animal's balance toward the horse's opposite side—in this case, more toward the horse's opposite hind leg. It can be used for a turn of very small radius or to collect and balance the horse back onto its haunches in a turn. There is actually a continuum of rein aids between the two indirect reins; the rider uses whichever variant (or whatever degree) is needed at that particular time.

Bearing or Neck Rein

Snaffle. One hand moves to (rarely, across) the horse's mane, laying the rein against the horse's neck. Crossing the horse's mane with the rein hand may result in a totally different signal than the rider intended and may be avoided by shortening the rein. This rein aid is used when the other rein is used in a direct, indirect, or leading manner, and this aid decreases the radius of the turn.

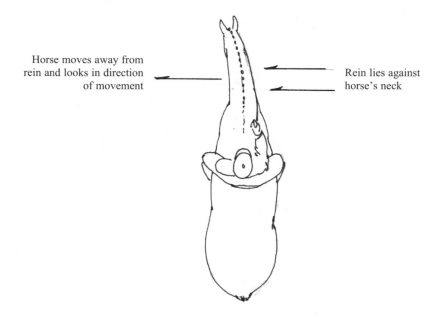

Horse moves away from rein and looks in direction of movement

Rein lies against horse's neck

16.3 Bearing or Neck Rein

Curb. This aid is the primary curb-bit turning rein aid. It results from the rider moving the rein hand laterally in the direction the individual wants to turn. The hand should not drop below the horse's crest.

General neck rein. In the bearing or neck rein aid, there is no backward pressure on the bit, although there may be contact. The horse moves away from the pressure of the rein as it bears against the animal's neck; the result may be a bend, a turn, or decreased radius of the turn. The neck rein has no power to actually bend the horse's neck; the horse must learn to bend its neck by association with earlier (in training) opening (or later, direct) rein use. The difference between the neck rein and the indirect reins is in the bend of the horse's neck: the horse bends toward the indirect reins and away from the neck rein.

Opening or Leading Rein

One hand, holding one rein, moves out to the side, leading the horse's nose to that side. The horse's body should follow. The opening or leading rein, named for the opening hand action and the leading of the horse's head, works very well with a snaffle, side-pull, or bosal hackamore but poorly with a curb. This is a useful rein aid for young horses that are just learning to turn their heads in the direction they are moving and for beginning riders. It is a very clear turning signal. It does not give the accuracy of the other turning methods; it does not prevent the horse from leaning into the turn or turning too sharply.

16.4 Opening or Leading Rein

Pulley Rein with Snaffle

This rein aid works only with snaffle bits. After shortening both reins, plant one hand firmly on the crest of the neck, right in front of the withers. You should feel a pull on the horse's mouth with this hand. Bring the other hand up and across the horse's neck toward your opposite chest with a strong pull.

This emergency brake will help you put extra pressure on the horse's mouth because you are actually pulling against the hand that is braced on the animal's neck. It is obviously a punishment and should only be used in an emergency after other correctly applied rein aids do not work. Be certain to sit deep and get your head back out of the way, because the horse will stop suddenly with its head up.

16.5 Pulley Rein

One-Rein Stop

The one-rein stop is used to stop the horse, and it can be used as an emergency brake. It also has a training purpose: it is used to disengage the hindquarters (stop using them for forward motion and displace them to the side). Its additional value includes softening and suppling the horse to the inside rein.

While the horse is walking, take the slack out of one rein (the left rein in diagram 16.6) and bring your hand toward your hip on that side. At the same time, apply the inside leg behind the girth/cinch. When you feel the horse begin to step sideways behind, release the leg and allow the horse to settle to a halt with its head softly drawn around toward your inside knee. As soon as the horse is softly yielding to the rein, release the pressure as a reward.

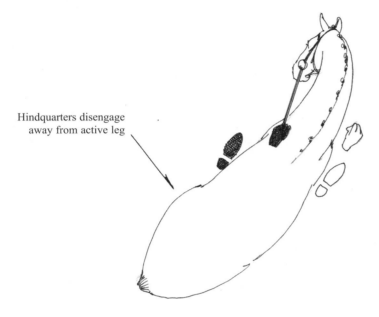

Hindquarters disengage
away from active leg

16.6 One-Rein Stop

NOTES

17

RIDING AT TROT AND CANTER

Three Ways to Ride Trot

The trot may be ridden in two-point position (discussed in detail in Chapter 13, Two-Point Position). This position is useful as an exercise for hunt- and stock-seat riders, while learning to jump, when riding a long-strided trot or over uneven ground, and when riding up steep hills.

The trot/jog may be ridden seated in the saddle, called sitting. Sitting the trot is more difficult for beginners than two point or posting, but as the rider's ability increases, faster and longer-strided trots can also be ridden sitting.

The third way to ride trot is to post or rise.

Posting the Trot

Posting is not permitted in western horse-show classes, but it is useful for riding across country and for any time the rider wants to ease the weight on the horse's back. It keeps the rider out of the horse's way when the horse is performing a springy trot and the rider's flexibility does not allow the individual to keep up. It is also helpful to the rider in dictating the rhythm of the horse's trot and to help the horse generate impulsion.

Posting is an up and forward and then down motion of the rider's hips. The rider rolls forward and then back on the inner thigh. The rider's shoulders are slightly ahead of the vertical and move very little.

The rein hand(s) stay low and close to the horse's neck. The beginning rider's reins are held long enough so that involuntary hand movements are not felt by the horse. There are different ways to remind the rider how to keep the hand(s) low and still: holding the mane, or using a neck strap (English) or keeping the hand near the horn (western). These positions prevent the common problem of hands that post with the rider's body. Under no circumstances will the reins (and therefore the horse's mouth) be used to help the rider balance.

The knees and heels sink down more than normal as the rider rises. This motion occurs because the weight previously borne by the seat now goes down through the knees, past the balls of the feet, and into the heels. This slight up-and-down knee and heel motion when the rider posts is desirable and will occur when the individual rides by balance instead of grip.

The rider simply inclines forward at the hips and lets the horse's movement push the individual out of the saddle. The rider holds the "up" position for one beat, then sinks gently back into the saddle (landing slightly more forward on the thighs and crotch than usual) for the next beat. A common problem with novice riders is the rider trying to heave oneself up out of the saddle. Given the correct leg and upper body position, the horse provides all the thrust necessary to roll the rider forward.

The trot is a two-beat gait in which the diagonal pairs of legs move together. The rider may rise with either pair of legs. From the saddle, the rider can see the point of the shoulder of the left foreleg move forward alternately with the point of the shoulder of the right foreleg. If the individual rises as the horse's left shoulder moves forward, the rider is posting on the left diagonal. If the rider rises as the horse's right shoulder moves forward, the individual is posting on the right diagonal.

See diagram 17.1 for an illustration of posting on the left diagonal. The diagram shows that the rider rises with the point of the left shoulder's forward movement; the individual is up when the point of the left shoulder is forward. The rider sinks when the point of the shoulder comes back so that the individual is sitting when the point of the left shoulder is back.

The correct diagonal is the outside one (near the arena rail or toward the outside of the turn).

Posting Diagonals

When changing direction or bend (whether in the arena or out in the open), the rider must change the posting diagonal. When riding long distances, the rider should change posting diagonals frequently to keep the horse moving evenly with both diagonal pairs of legs. Changing the posting diagonal is accomplished by staying down an extra beat: up, down, up, down, down, up, down, up.

The Canter/Lope

The three-beat canter is comfortable to sit after the rider gets the feel of this rolling gait. Lope can be ridden more easily by a novice. When you first learn to canter, you may find it easier to ride it in two-point position. As you get the feel of the gait, practice sitting down.

Your lower back must be very supple in order to absorb the shock of the horse's movements. In order to follow the horse's motion, your pelvis will tilt forward and back in rhythm with the animal's strides. The feeling is a faster version of the way you feel while pushing a park swing to make it go higher.

Your knees and ankles must stay bent and flexible for further shock absorption. You will find it easier to keep your seat in the saddle if you let your knees open slightly wider than normal as the horse's body comes up under you. This position will allow you to sit rather than rise when the horse does. Your ankles flex to allow your heels to move down and up a little as you have

The rider rises so that the individual is up when the point of the left shoulder is forward.

The rider sinks so that the individual is sitting when the left shoulder is back.

17.1 Posting on the Left Diagonal

more or less weight in your heels. Your toes will also make little horizontal circles as the horse's sides push your legs in and out. During a hunt-seat canter, your upper body moves forward and back slightly as your hip angle opens and closes slightly. From the side, your body will be between the vertical position of sitting trot and the more forward position of rising trot. At a slow lope, your upper body moves less and you can stay more vertical. Your eyes and head are up. Your shoulders are relaxed, allowing your arms to hang down naturally and move forward and back with the horse's neck. Your elbows stay bent and supple so they can both open and close. Your wrists are straight, yet flexible, and your hands are closed. The horse moves its head and neck more at canter than at walk or trot, and you have to be supple to be able to follow this motion.

Canter/Lope Leads

One side of the horse's body "leads" the other as the animal canters. In the sequence of footfalls, the legs on the leading side are extended farther forward than those on the other side. The horse is best balanced on turns if its inside legs lead.

17.2 The Right Legs Leading in Right-Lead Canter/Lope

Canter/Lope Aids

This section is meant to supplement your instructor's instructions; there are many ways of signaling for these gaits, and it is best to use the method your horse is familiar with. In order of simple to complex, common methods of signaling for canter/lope follow.

Outside lateral aids. Your instructor may ask you to use the outside leg most strongly and turn the horse's nose to the outside (with a snaffle) or neck rein out (with a curb). The active outside hand (with a snaffle) and leg gives this method its "lateral" title.

Usually the dominant part of the canter/lope signal is the rider's outside leg used behind the girth/cinch. Behind the girth/cinch means that the leg is stretched backward, both from the hip and by bending the knee slightly, and used four to six inches behind where it normally lies. The outside heel is not raised, nor is the calf brought up toward the horizontal when the leg is stretched back.

Diagonal aids (with snaffle). This method involves an active outside leg (behind the girth/cinch) and inside hand (turning the horse's nose in but preventing the horse from turning). This method is called diagonal aids because of the relationship of the two active aids.

Outside leg, horse's nose to inside. This aid is the neck-reining version of the above method. The outside leg is the dominant leg, and the horse's nose is tipped slightly toward the inside (lead side). You may be able to accomplish this movement with a slight neck rein or use the inside curb rein to tip the head in. The first finger or little finger can be used on the inside rein to shorten it slightly and cue the horse.

All aids in use. Experienced riders have both hands (unless riding western with one hand when they use one hand to manipulate the reins individually) and both legs to influence the horse to take the correct canter lead. The outside leg is back and active. The inside leg remains in its normal hanging position but comes in to contact the horse's side as needed. This cueing position is called "at the cinch/girth" or "on the cinch/girth," though it actually makes contact with the horse's side at the back edge of the cinch/girth. (It is the same position as used to signal for walk or trot.) When active, the inside leg balances the horse, keeps the animal from moving to the inside, keeps the horse's slight bend to the inside, and encourages the horse to go forward. The reins influence the horse to look slightly to the inside, consistent with the position of canter/lope, but not lean or move inward. Having the potential to use both reins and both legs in any combination and at any instant gives the rider the chance to best choose the lead and shape the canter/lope.

General Canter/Lope Explanation

Once the horse takes a stride (one three-beat sequence of footfalls) of canter/lope, you may need to use both your legs to encourage the horse to stay in the gait. Your cues are dependent on the horse's actions; if the horse takes the gait energetically, you may not need to encourage the animal; alternately, you may need to use the aids strongly. Regardless, keep your calves close and ready in order to be able to use them at any time as necessary.

The first few times cantering may be easier on the horse's back and mouth and more comfortable for the rider if the rider rests one or both hands on the horse's neck (English) or the free hand on the horn (western). Your instructor will advise you. If this is the case, the reins will need to be shortened, because the horse raises its head and shortens its neck in canter. However, some slack must remain in the reins. If both hands rest on the neck, one or the other hand is lifted for direct or opening rein steering.

As the rider progresses, the individual is able to keep the hands steady during the transition to canter/lope. Then the rider can add the appropriate rein aids to the leg aids. The reins are used just prior to the leg aids to position the horse's head and neck in the direction of the lead. With a snaffle, the inside rein positions the head and neck to the inside, while the outside rein limits the amount of bend and steadies the forehand of the horse. With a curb, the outside rein is used as a neck rein to bring the forehand slightly to the inside.

Checking for Correct Canter/Lope Lead

The goal is to eventually be able to determine if the horse is on the correct lead by feel. In the meantime, check the lead by glancing down at the horse's shoulders where they join the neck. The inside shoulder should be moving farther forward than the outside. This movement shows that the horse is on the correct lead.

The best time to be looking down with your eyes is during the third beat of the stride. The third beat is easy to recognize; it is at this time that you feel most firmly down in the saddle. Also at this time, the difference in shoulder position is most obvious. However, this timing will only come with practice. At first, many strides will be watched.

If the horse is cantering/loping on the wrong lead, the animal is brought back to a comfortable trot, walk, or halt, and the correct aids are used again.

Checking for Correct Diagonals or Leads

When glancing down to check your diagonal or the horse's lead, do it quickly. Practice until you can tell at a glance; this quick glance enables you to look up and see where you are going for the maximum amount of time. Do not be obvious about checking. Look down with just your eyes, and keep your head up. Moving your head changes your balance and can lead to rounded shoulders and a collapsed chest. Your eventual goal is to not have to look down at all; practice until you can pick up your diagonals and detect the horse's leads by feel.

The Difference between Diagonals and Leads

Do not confuse posting diagonals with canter/lope leads. Diagonals are performed by the rider when the horse trots. The rider is correct to post with the horse's outside shoulder. The individual sits an extra beat to change diagonals.

Leads are performed by the horse at canter/lope/gallop. The horse may be correct or incorrect. The correct lead is the inside one. It is the rider's responsibility to ask for the correct lead and then check to make sure it is correct. If the horse is on the wrong lead, the rider signals the horse to change the lead with a simple or flying change of lead.

NOTES

18
ARENA LETTERS

Riding arenas are sometimes labeled with letters; these letters are displayed on the walls or fence around the perimeter. The purposes of the letters are to identify divisions of the arena (for example, show the halfway point along one side) and to identify where in the arena a movement is to be executed.

While the sequence of the letters comes from dressage traditions and is international in use, history does not give any reason for the letters chosen. Since there seems to be no pattern to the letters, the use of a mnemonic is probably the best way to remember where the letters are. An example of a mnemonic is using the first letters of the words "A Killer Elephant Has Caught My Best Friend." Knowing that A is located midway along one short side and that you proceed clockwise with this mnemonic, you will remember that K, E, and H are along one long side, C is the midpoint of the other short side, and M, B, and F label the other long side. The letter X, while usually not displayed, designates the center of the arena. Another common mnemonic is "A Fat Bay Mare Can Hardly Ever Kick." This mnemonic is used counterclockwise.

The imaginary line from C to A is called the center line. The two lines parallel to the center line are quarter lines. The B to E line is called the mid line. The K-E-H and F-B-M sides are sometimes called long sides, while the C and A sides are called short sides.

When riding along the rail or track (parallel to and close to the arena fence), you are either tracking right (moving clockwise; the command is "track right") or tracking left (moving counterclockwise; the command is "track left"). The terms can be remembered in at least two ways: "track right" means that your right hand is to the inside, while "track left" means that your left hand is in; track right means to ride from the middle of the arena and, when reaching the rail, turn right, while the opposite is true for track left.

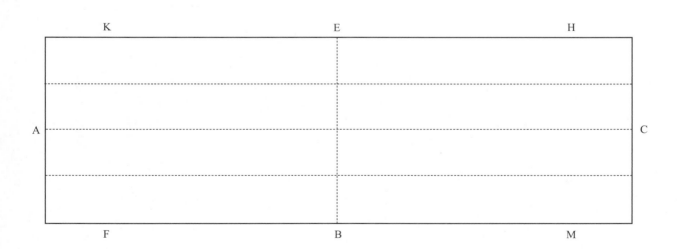

18.1 Arena Letters

NOTES

ARENA FIGURES

Arena figures are patterns that you ride to practice your aids and improve your accuracy, and when a number of riders are using the same space, these figures lend predictability and order to the session. These figures help make the horse more supple (flexible) laterally (from side to side), help the animal's balance, and check the horse's obedience. There are many such patterns; your instructor will likely have some favorites, and there are patterns common to different riding disciplines. Your instructor will prescribe suitable patterns for your ability. The arena figures in this chapter are common to the dressage discipline and, as they are a good basis for any type of riding, may be part of your lessons.

These patterns may be executed almost anywhere in the arena. If your arena is labeled with letters, your instructor may ask you to execute a certain pattern starting at a certain letter and possibly finishing at the same or another letter. The examples here show common places of execution; these places are not by any means the only suitable locations.

The size of the figure makes it more or less difficult; larger patterns are usually easier for both you and the horse. The sizes shown here are standard for a standard-size dressage arena (20 by 60 meters). Your instructor may want you to ride patterns of a certain size to show your control; if so, these patterns are offered as suggestions.

Most of the figures pictured in the following diagrams may be ridden in either direction (which is why there are no arrows or the arrows do not specify a single direction). A few diagrams have arrows to better describe the example, while other figures (like the half circles) must be ridden in the direction shown, or they become another figure.

Some figures cause you to change the direction you are traveling on the rail, and others involve changes of direction within the figure. Changes of direction challenge your aids and the horse's balance.

When riding on a straight line, the horse's body should be straight from nose to tail, and your body and aids should be even. When riding on a curved line, the horse's body should be curved from nose to tail corresponding to the radius of the turn, and your body and aids will correspond to the horse's bend.

Each figure should be practiced and perfected at the walk before being ridden at the trot/jog, and when perfected at the trot/jog, some figures may then be cantered/loped.

Circles

Circles are round figures that start and end at the same point. They are easiest to ride if you mentally divide them in half and calculate the halfway point. For example, the large circle at B in diagram 19.1 takes the entire width of the arena. Its halfway point is E, and you will ride the second half the same size as the first half.

The smaller circles at E and A in diagram 19.1 are half the width of the arena in size. Notice that the center line provides a convenient halfway point for any circle of this size that happens to start on either long side of the arena.

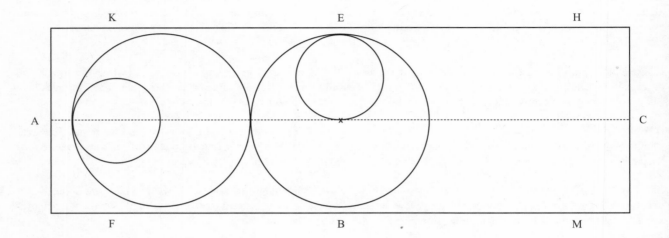

19.1 Circles

Half Circles

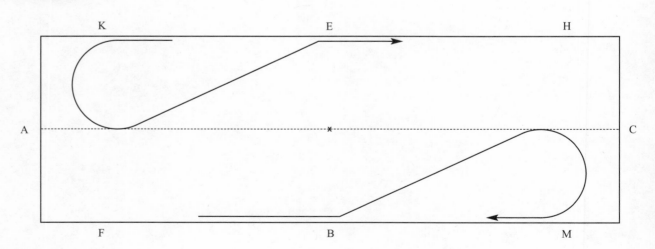

Half Circle at K, Returning to the Track at E, and
Half Circle in Reverse at B, Returning to the Track at M

19.2 Half Circles

These figures consist of half a circle of the designated size plus a diagonal line that is tangent to the halfway point of the circle. Both the half circle and the half circle in reverse will result in a change of direction.

The half circle begins with half a circle and is completed by riding a straight diagonal line back to the rail. The half circle shown in diagram 19.2 begins at K, ends at E, and has a diameter of half the width of the arena.

The half circle in reverse, shown in diagram 19.2 starting at B, begins with a diagonal line and ends with a half circle. Half circles in reverse are more challenging to ride than half circles.

When trotting or cantering/loping half circles, you will need to change your posting diagonal or the horse's lead. The change occurs in the half circle as you return to the rail (at E in diagram 19.2). During a half circle in reverse, the change of diagonal or lead is made as you leave the rail (shown at B in the diagram 19.2).

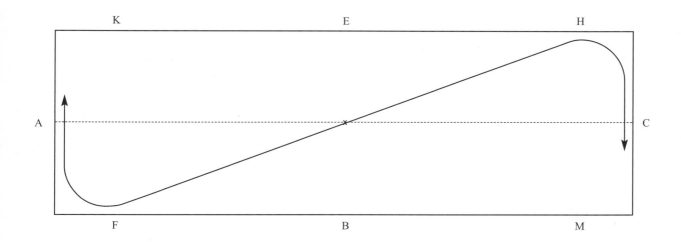

19.3 Diagonal Change of Rein (Direction)

Diagonal Change of Rein (Direction)

A change of rein (direction) across a diagonal may begin at H or F when tracking left, and it may begin at K or M when tracking right. Remember to always ride around the short side of the arena before beginning the diagonal; if you start too soon (at the letter before a short side), you will have to make a difficult, sharp turn to begin the diagonal. If your instructor asks for a change of rein in a marked arena, you will likely be told what letters to follow. For example, diagram 19.3 shows a change of rein from H, through X, and to F, called "H-X-F." This diagonal may also be ridden, as the arrows show, beginning track left, "F-X-H."

To ride a smooth, accurate pattern, look for the ending letter as you enter the first corner. Bring the horse smoothly off the track as your shoulder passes the starting letter. Continue to look across the diagonal at the ending letter, so you ride a straight line. Plan to return to the track just before you reach the letter, so you are on the track as your shoulder passes the letter. Continue smoothly around the corner. If you are in doubt as to which way to turn at the end of the diagonal, go the direction that will give you the easiest, widest turn. You have changed the direction you are traveling on the track.

If the horse is trotting and you are posting, remember to change your posting diagonal at X. If the horse is cantering/loping, a change of lead is usually executed at X: bring the horse to trot/jog or walk and cue for the other lead.

Three-Loop Serpentine

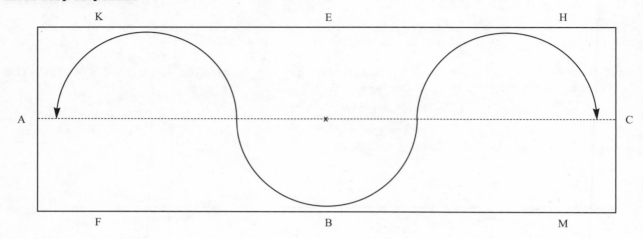

19.4 Three-Loop Serpentine, Half-Circle Pattern

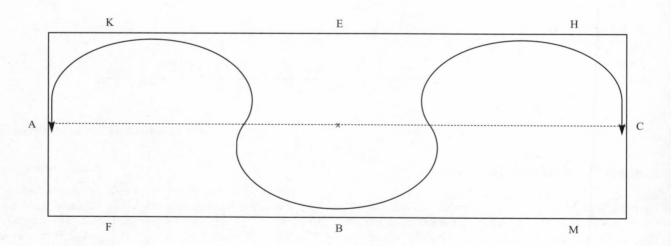

19.5 Three-Loop Serpentine, Pronounced Change-of-Bend Pattern

Serpentines consist of a number of even, rounded loops. In dressage patterns, they traditionally begin at A or C and end at the letter on the opposite end of the center line. For example, you may be asked for a "three-loop serpentine from C to A".

To ride a serpentine, mentally divide the arena into as many sections as there will be loops. Each loop takes up one section; the loop begins and ends on the center line. Ride each loop as a smooth curve that intersects the track at its halfway point.

Beginning horses and riders should make serpentines with a straight line as long as possible on either side of the center line. (See diagram 19.6; an even longer straight line is possible) This method is the easiest way to ride the figure; it gives you as much time as possible to organize the horse and change the bend. As horse and rider advance, the loops can be made with shorter straight sections (see diagram 19.4). When working on changing canter/lope leads, you can make the curves more pronounced (see diagram 19.5). This pattern gives you a well-defined change of bend near the center line, which helps with the lead change.

106

Four-Loop Serpentine

Three- and four-loop serpentines are the most common. Notice that a three-loop pattern (or any serpentine consisting of an odd number of loops) will take you back to the track in the same direction you started. Serpentines with an even number of loops will cause you to change the direction you were originally traveling on the rail.

Each loop requires you and the horse to look and turn the opposite way from the previous loop. The change occurs as you cross the center line. If the horse is trotting and you are posting, you should change your posting diagonal each time you cross the center line and turn the opposite way. If the horse is cantering/loping, you must bring the horse down to trot/jog or walk and cue the animal to take the opposite lead.

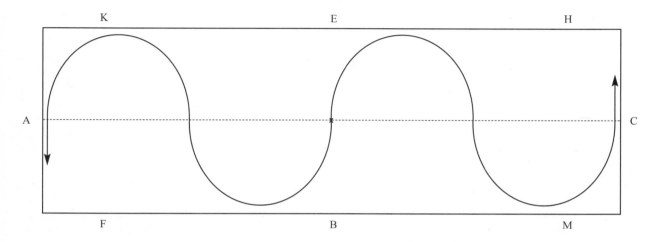

19.6 Four-Loop Serpentine, Straight-across-Centerline Pattern

Figure Eight

A figure eight, in dressage, reining, and equitation disciplines, is made up of two loops that join at one point. This pattern may be ridden with large or small circles and in different locations in the arena. The center point is both beginning and end, and halfway through the pattern, the horse changes direction through the center point. Care must be taken to plan ahead and ride accurately. The circles must be the same size. The center point must be at the same place in the arena each time you ride through it. Use objects along the rail to guide you. Remember to change posting diagonals or leads as you change direction.

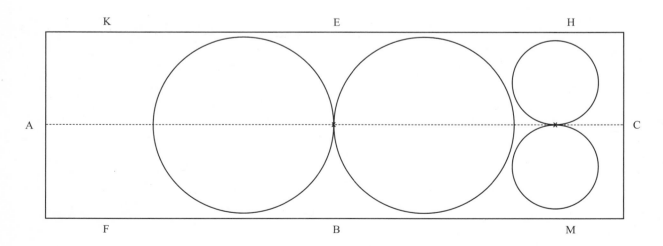

19.7 Figure Eight

Change of Rein within the Circle

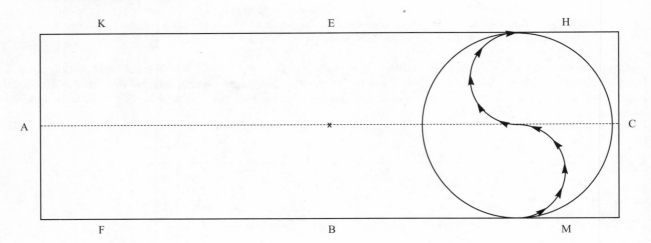

19.8 Change of Rein within the Circle

After riding at least once around any adequately sized circle, you can make a smooth change of direction within that circle. Ride smoothly off the rail and bend in until you reach the center point, and then change the horse's bend and make a similar curve the other direction. You should finish out on the original circle at a point exactly opposite your starting point. Remember to change your posting diagonal or the horse's canter/lope lead at the center of the change. The diagram shows a change of direction from tracking left to tracking right.

RIDING TURNS AND CORNERS

In the early stages of riding, much of the rider's concentration is on balance; the student is taught just enough about steering to get the horse from one place to another (and sometimes not very accurately!). As the student progresses, the individual's balance and coordination get better, and more subtle aids can be used to get more subtle and correct results. The rider is able to feel and interpret more of what the horse is doing. Interpretation does not always come with the ability to act on what the horse is doing, though. Aid coordination takes time to develop, and improved balance in the saddle increases effectiveness of the aids.

This chapter describes the use of the reins and legs in riding turns and corners and is organized in approximately the order that a rider might learn the aid combinations. This chapter emphasizes the snaffle bit, since many western riders (plus hunt- and saddle-seat riders) are first taught to ride with a snaffle.

Pressure and Release

The horse is trained to respond to pressure on its mouth, neck, sides, etc. When pressure is applied, the rider must wait a second or two for a response and then reward the response by ceasing the pressure. If the horse fails to respond or resists, the pressure is increased or varied; the correct response must be elicited or else the horse is being taught that the pressure does not mean that it must respond.

Horse Body Position

In a turn or corner (excepting spins, barrel racing turns, etc.) the horse's body should be curved from head to tail along the track over which the animal moves. This curve is necessary because of the way the horse balances; if the animal is not curved, or worse is curved in the opposite direction, it will lean in instead. Small turns should be made with more curve in the body than large turns. The curve is evident in the way the neck is bent and in the tracks of the hooves; there is a small amount of lateral flexibility through the horse's back.

The rider should eventually control both the horse's head/neck and the hindquarters. When bending the horse, the reins influence the forehand while the legs control the hindquarters. On a turn of radius shown in Chapter 19, Arena Figures, the horse is looking inward correctly if the rider can glance down and see the rear corner of the horse's inside eye. The correct tracking of the hindquarters is visible from the ground; the instructor may help the student learn both to see the tracking in other students' horses and to feel it in the individual's own horse.

Rein Aids

Rein aids serve as directional, bending, speed, and collection/extension signals. The student will progress from concentrating on one hand (or leg) aid at a time to being able to use all the aids, simultaneously or in succession, as needed.

Two-Leg Positions

The legs are used independently of each other (as the rider progresses) in both strength of signal and in position.

The position in which the leg normally hangs (at the rear edge of the girth or cinch) is called at the girth/cinch. Leg(s) in this position are used to keep the horse moving, to keep the animal from decreasing the size of the turn, and to create or retain the bend.

The position approximately four to six inches behind this position is called behind the girth/cinch. It is attained by stretching the leg back from the hip and keeping the heel low (not by bending the knee and raising the heel). The ankle is kept supple to avoid losing the stirrup. This aid influences the track of the hindquarters, is part of the aids for canter/lope depart, and contributes to impulsion.

The legs can also be used in conjunction with the rein aids to create collection in the horse and to move the horse laterally. Neither method will be discussed in this book.

Rider's Eyes

Always look up, ahead, and toward where you want the horse to go. This practice means looking through a corner or halfway around a circle. Looking up helps keep your body in balance. Looking ahead helps you plan your path. Turning your eyes and head balances you and gives subtle directional cues to the horse.

Steady Hands

Steady hand(s) that work independently of your body are the ideal. Your instructor will tell you (and you will be able to feel) when your hands are unsteady. Unsteady hands can give unintentional tugs on the horse's mouth and act as unintentional signals (which the horse may react to or learn to ignore) or even be abusive. While it is possible to concentrate and steady your hand(s) even while your body is stiff, unbalanced, or bouncing, the ideal is to stabilize your body first by developing the proper position, flexibility, strength, and balance. As your riding improves, you will be able to be more steady and then more independent with your hands. Steady hands allow you to take the slack out of your reins and give subtle, sensitive rein aids.

While you are learning to ride and concentrating on your position or balance, there are times when your hands will move unintentionally. Your instructor will be able to help you keep from confusing or hurting the horse. There are many techniques you can use. Slowing down is one. If the horse's neck is within reach, you can place the knuckles of your rein hand(s) on it at an appropriate distance from the withers or you can hold a handful of mane with the rein(s). A properly adjusted (lengthwise) neck strap can be held with the rein hand(s) on horses with high head carriage. The horn or swells can be held with the free hand when learning in a western saddle.

Inside Leading or Direct Rein and Both Legs Signal a Turn

Beginning riders using snaffles often learn to turn the horse initially with the inside leading rein and then progress to the use of the inside direct rein. Both methods involve the use of one (active) hand at a time, so they are relatively easy to execute. Both aids are simple and clear to the horse; they encourage the animal to follow its nose.

The other (outside) hand is passive, or yields forward if the horse needs more rein; this yielding makes the signal clearer to the horse (the animal responds to the one rein it feels and is not confused into stopping).

Although not perfected until a later developmental stage, the rider soon learns that the outside snaffle rein, shortened, can be used to limit the bend of the horse's neck. For example, the left rein can be used on a turn to the right to keep the horse from bending its neck too far to the right. This use of the outside snaffle rein establishes more control over the size of the turn.

Both of the rider's legs are used as necessary to squeeze and release, tap, or kick in order to keep the horse moving forward at the same gait through the turn. Both legs are used initially on the horse's barrel without any displacement of the outside leg to the rear.

Neck Reining—Snaffle or Curb

The outside snaffle rein can be used by a more experienced rider as a neck rein by bringing the hand in toward the neck, but not across the crest, and laying the rein against the side of the neck. This neck rein is an additional turning signal for the horse; it signals the turn and can decrease the radius of the turn.

Using a curb bit, the rider neck reins by bringing the hand holding the reins across the horse's neck. The feel of the outside rein on its neck signals the trained horse to turn its nose and move the opposite direction. If the horse does not respond, inexperienced riders may try to pull the reins more tightly across the neck. This movement can be very confusing to the horse, because it can actually point the animal's head the wrong direction for the turn.

Preventing Cutting In—Basic Snaffle Use

Most horses will try to "cut" corners in the arena and to cut off the last part of a circle. This cutting is prevented, assuming it is anticipated, by the beginner with the use of the outside leading (snaffle) rein. The disadvantage of this novice solution is that the horse looks to the outside of the turn (which may put the animal off balance), and the horse can still cut in onto the inside shoulder (see diagram 20.1). The addition of the inside leg, used in the position it hangs (at the girth/cinch), will strengthen the signal to keep the horse out and help preserve the bend to the inside.

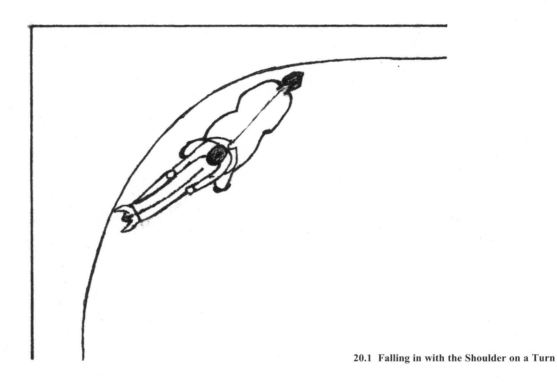

20.1 Falling in with the Shoulder on a Turn

Inside Aids to Enlarge the Turn

There is another rein aid, combined with the inside leg, that will enlarge a turn without bending the horse incorrectly to the outside: the inside indirect rein in front of the withers and inside leg used on the girth/cinch. Using a snaffle, the rider brings the inside hand inward at the angle for an indirect rein. Using a curb bit, the rider brings the hand slightly back and to the outside; bringing the hand back brings the inside rein into effect as an indirect rein. The inside indirect rein, used properly, is very effective in keeping the horse's head to the inside while keeping the animal's shoulders out. This signal tells the horse to carry more of its weight on its outside foreleg and makes it easier for the animal to enlarge the turn. The indirect rein works only if the rider has a feel of the horse's mouth, so it can be used only at gaits in which the rider demonstrates steady hands (walk only, at first).

The inside indirect snaffle rein may be used with an outside opening rein. Moving the outside hand out helps enlarge the turn the forehand is making. Be sure not to use such a strong opening rein that the horse looks to the outside.

As always, the reins influence the forehand while the rider's legs control the hindquarters. The inside leg used at the girth/cinch is a strong helper for the indirect rein aid; it signals the horse to shift its weight toward the outside, move away from the leg aid, and retain its body bend toward the inside. The inside leg is also very useful in keeping the horse moving forward through turns and can be used alone or with the outside leg for this purpose. If you are using the inside leg both to push the horse out and to energize the animal and if you want to use your outside leg also to keep the horse going, be certain your outside leg is used behind the girth, not at it, so it does not contradict the lateral power of the inside leg that you are using at the girth/cinch.

Keeping the Hindquarters in with the Outside Leg

The hindquarters do not always follow the forehand around a turn as they should; sometimes they take an outside track (see diagram 20.2). The rider's outside leg used behind the girth/cinch signals the horse to follow the tracks of the forefeet with the hind feet.

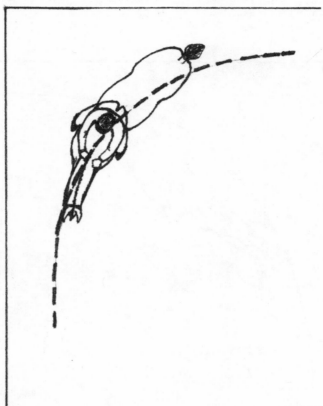

20.2 **Hindquarters Swinging out on a Turn**

All Aids in Use

Riders are constantly feeling what the horse is doing and making corrections. Riding involves deciding what you want the horse to do, asking for that action, and continually shaping the animal's movements. The best results come from anticipating what the horse may do and signaling the animal to do what you desire instead. The ability to correct a horse comes with time and practice.

The rein and leg aids chosen for a balanced turn will depend on the horse's balance and energy at every different moment; one set of aids will often be alternated or exchanged with another. The goal is to use both legs and both reins in harmony to get the desired effect.

21

BEGINNING JUMPING

Learning to ride over fences in a hunt-seat saddle is very much like learning to ride on the flat in some ways. Both skills require that you ride in a balanced position: at first, you concentrate on your balance while the horse does simple, routine exercises. Later you will be able to concentrate on the horse and progress to more challenging exercises for you both.

A big part of the instructor's job is to present exercises of ever-increasing difficulty that challenge but do not overwhelm or endanger the rider. The presence of an instructor cannot be overemphasized. Do not jump, even cavalletti, alone or unsupervised. The student is encouraged to ask questions and seek answers; the rider is ultimately responsible for one's own progress.

An approved safety helmet must be worn while jumping; it is recommended for flat riding, too, regardless of the style of riding.

Before you start jumping, you must master certain things. You must be able to keep the lesson horse at an even pace in trot and canter. You must be able to balance in two-point position at trot and canter. You may need to press your knuckles into the horse's neck or hold the mane while jumping, but your two-point position must be stable enough for you to take your hands off the neck and steer between jumps. You must be able to get, and keep, a line of sight; in other words, you must be able to focus your eyes on a specified point and ride straight to it.

Rider's Position

Two-point position. When you first learn to jump, your instructor may have you ride in two-point position before, during, and after the jump. Two-point position keeps you balanced and keeps you from interfering with the horse (keeps your weight off the animal's back) until you learn to follow the horse's movements. You will hold the mane when necessary.

The horse can carry you over the jump if you are sitting down in the saddle, but the animal loses some of its freedom of movement. The horse's back and neck should arch (bascule) over the fence. Sitting down on the horse's back over the jump may cause the animal to jump flat (no bascule) or inverted (arched upside down) or to hit the jump with its hind legs.

Upper-body position. Your hip angle will be more closed over a jump than it was in two-point position. The more effort the horse makes, the more your hip angle closes. This position is necessary to keep you in balance as the horse's balance changes.

It is important to realize that you do not make your upper body go forward from two-point position as the horse jumps. If you try to anticipate the thrust and lean forward, you are likely to throw yourself off balance. You may even get ahead of the horse and cause or allow the animal to stop. Instead, stay supple and let the horse's movement close your hip angle as the animal takes off for the jump.

Hand position. The position and suppleness of the rider's hands are important for the horse's freedom and comfort and for the rider's balance and control. Eventually, when the horse is well balanced and educated, the rider will follow the horse's mouth over the fence, keeping light contact throughout. Beginners are not well balanced enough to follow the horse's mouth in the air over a jump. A pull or jerk on the horse's mouth at any time during the jumping effort is punishment that, if repeated, may cause the horse to refuse to jump. Therefore, beginning jumpers keep their balance and keep their hands from interfering by moving their hands forward and pressing their knuckles into the crest of the horse's neck. The hands are usually between one-third and halfway up the horse's neck, making somewhat loose reins. The rider may hold mane with one hand. This hand position is called a crest release. A release frees the horse's head, neck, and mouth; one mark of a correct release is that it accommodates the horse's need for freedom at that time.

When jumping for the first few times, the rider places the hands on the neck before reaching the jump. Later the individual moves the hands to this position as the horse jumps. Later still, the rider releases onto the crest but does not hold the mane except during an awkward jump. As the rider's balance improves, the student can place the hands closer to the body and thus take most of the slack out of the reins. This placement gives more control. The most advanced rider does an automatic release by following the horse's mouth down and forward, keeping contact all the time. This position allows maximum communication and control.

Learning to Jump

Stage 1. As soon as the rider can balance in two-point position at the trot, trotting poles are introduced. The first step is to trot over one pole on the ground, practicing two point and the crest release. Practice riding a straight line up to, over, and away from the pole. At first, you must ride a steady horse so you can concentrate on your position and not on rating the horse.

The next step is to ride over four or five ground poles spaced 4 feet apart. (This spacing is an average distance; your instructor will see to it that your poles are set correctly for your horse's stride.) The horse should put one front foot (and one hind foot) between each pole and trot through in a steady rhythm. These poles are called cavalletti. They may be raised off the ground, causing the horse to pick up its feet more and be more energetic. They may be spaced at varying, yet regular, distances. The poles may be set on a straight or curved track. Cavalletti, with their many possible arrangements, are invaluable for teaching both riders and horses. Cavalletti accustom the rider to more springy movement of the horse. Depending on the exercise, the horse may or may not jump over them. Cavalletti give the rider a chance to practice a straight, steady approach without added height or jumping effort.

Stage 2. The next stage is to trot the cavalletti and then a cross-rail spaced approximately 9 feet after the last cavalletti. Cross-rails are jumps with two rails crossed in the middle so that the lowest point is in the middle; cross-rails encourage the horse and rider to cross the center of the jump. This exercise is good to practice after your balance and position are steady at Stage 1. You will need more spring in your shock absorbers—ankles and knees—and better, more dynamic balance for Stage 2. Do not make the mistake of standing up or jumping with the horse; let the animal do the work. You merely stay softly in two-point position; your hip angle closes as the horse jumps. You may practice the crest-release exercise (see Chapter 14, Rider Exercises on Horseback) to help your hip angle stay supple.

A variation on the second stage exercise is a single pole placed 9 feet in front of the cross-rail, with no cavalletti. (This distance and others mentioned here may be changed to accommodate different horses' stride lengths.) The ground pole helps set the horse's takeoff distance and, like the cavalletti, encourages the horse to trot all the way to the fence.

Stay at this stage, riding a number of different horses, until you are well balanced and confident.

Stage 3. The third stage involves cantering to a fence, but in a controlled situation so that the takeoff for the canter fence is smooth. Most often, this procedure is accomplished by trotting to one fence, landing cantering, and cantering a second fence that is a calculated and measured distance away. The measured distance will ensure that the horse takes off after an even, balanced stride. Cantering fences is more difficult than trotting them. The horse can comfortably take off for the jump at two points in the trot stride. The canter stride, however, is longer and cannot be easily divided; it allows a comfortable takeoff at only one point in the sequence of footfalls.

There is an imaginary triangle-shaped takeoff zone in front of each fence (particularly fences with some width to them); the base of the triangle is parallel to the fence. A takeoff from this zone will allow the horse to comfortably clear the obstacle. At first, all your approaches to the fence will be at a right angle to the fence. This angle allows the maximum length of suitable takeoff area. Later as you advance to angled approaches, you must be more accurate in your approach, because the suitable takeoff zone is narrower.

If the horse gets to the comfortable takeoff phase of canter while the animal is in the takeoff zone, the fence will ride smoothly. If, however, the horse is ready to take off too soon or too late, the animal must adjust its stride to compensate. This difference in stride length is felt by the rider and can be made smooth only after much practice trotting into fences.

A combination of two fences, set no, one, or two strides apart, is called an in-and-out. Multiple fences spaced no, one, or two strides apart for practice are termed a gymnastic. A set of three fences in the show ring is usually referred to as a triple or a triple combination. Fences spaced three or more strides apart without turns in between are called a line.

Stage 4. This stage has the rider cantering the approaches to fences. The takeoff spot will not always work out well, but the rider's balance is good enough to prevent the individual's being left behind on an early takeoff or being tipped forward on a short stride before the takeoff.

At this stage, the rider should practice keeping a steady, even pace. The instructor will help with the speed; the ideal pace is the one that lets the horse stay balanced and meet the fences well. The horse is more likely to reach the fences correctly from a steady pace. As the rider gets the feel of how much ground these even strides consume, the individual will begin to develop an eye so that eventually the rider can see whether the horse will reach the fence on a comfortable stride or not. The next stage involves making adjustments in the horse's stride early in the approach so as to meet the fence correctly.

TRAIL RIDING

Riding outside over uneven terrain and around natural obstacles is fun! It may be your usual activity or can be a welcome break from arena work for you and your horse. Make trail riding a safe learning experience by following these guidelines. See also Chapter 24, Hill Work.

Before you start, check your horse's shoes. A shoe that loosens during an arena ride is not the same logistical problem as one that loosens on a many-mile trail ride. If your horse is barefoot, plan to travel over appropriate terrain.

It is better to ride with at least one other rider than to ride alone in case you need help. If you must ride alone, let someone know where you are going and when you expect to return. See also Chapter 23, Trail Riding with a Group.

It is a good idea if you will be a distance from the barn to carry a simple first-aid kit including items of immediate nature like a human bandage and a hoof pick (in case your horse picks up a rock). In areas where downed wire fences may be encountered, it is a good idea to carry wire cutters. A cellular telephone can get help when needed; consider carrying it on your body in case you part company with your horse, but avoid carrying it on the back of your belt where you might hurt your back if you should fall on it.

If there is any chance of the weather getting wet or cold while you are out, carry a rain coat or jacket. Tie it securely to the saddle where it will not flap in the breeze. The safest way to put on or take off a jacket is to dismount, make the change, and then remount. Putting on or taking off a jacket while riding is risky, because you have less control of the horse and the animal may object to the noise or motion of the coat.

Mount in the open, on grass, on dirt or gravel (avoid concrete and asphalt), away from overhangs and objects with protruding edges, and away from other horses.

Horses that do not get outside often may act very differently (more enthusiastically!) than they do indoors or in an arena. Take this possibility into account in your planning. Avoid getting your horse excited by speed work, particularly in a direction that might make the animal think it is going back to the barn (even if you are still some distance away, the horse knows where home is!). Horses learn quickly to run back to the barn and will often become unmanageable after just a few such runs.

Plan your ride so you can return in plenty of time to walk the last mile or so back to the barn. This walk cools out the horse while getting the horse in the habit of walking home.

Train ahead of time for water crossings, and use common sense when choosing places to cross. If the weather is hot, be sure the horse gets enough to drink during the ride. Be alert for pawing and that sinking feeling that your horse is going down in the water to roll—quickly use your aids to get the horse moving forward again.

Look ahead and watch for low branches, protruding bushes, and tree trunks. The horse allows enough room for its body, but you must steer to be sure there is enough room for your head and knees.

Keep your speed appropriate for the footing. It is up to you to keep your horse at a safe speed over rough ground, in mud or boggy spots, on snow, on pavement, or going down hills. When in doubt, walk; if you are unsure of the footing, it may be best to go around the area. Look ahead for footing changes, so you can slow down early. If you abruptly slow down in mud, you can cause the horse to slip and possibly strain a ligament or tendon. Cantering across an open field or loping through the trees is safer if you have first walked the route to check for new holes, muddy spots, or downed branches.

When crossing roads, stop to listen and look both ways before walking across. Choose the safest side of the road to ride on, given the shoulder situation, visibility for motorists, and how your horse may react to traffic. Ride in an alert fashion, and keep your horse in control when vehicles approach.

The horse that eats along the trail will make very slow progress and can choose inappropriate times to stop and eat. Eating during the ride is considered a bad habit in a horse unless you are training for competitive trail or endurance rides. Discourage eating by raising the horse's head with the rein(s) and using your leg aids to make the animal move along. It will be easier to condition the horse not to eat if you never let it eat while you are mounted. For example, choosing to let the horse eat while standing still but not while you are moving might be hard to enforce and confusing for the horse.

When riding near a field of pastured horses, the loose horses are likely to be curious and come over to investigate you. Stay out of their reach and keep moving. Avoid riding in the same enclosure with loose horses if at all possible until you are an experienced rider, as the loose horses may get your horse overly excited or come too close and cause a kicking accident.

Leave gates the way you found them (leave open ones open). Close any that you open, being sure to latch them securely.

Be alert but relaxed. As you ride, your horse will notice objects along the trail. Steady your horse if a new object bothers the animal. Look past it, and use your legs to push the horse right by. If you stare at the object, too, and tense up, the horse is more likely to stop or shy.

On a long ride, if you get tired or sore, get off and walk for a while (or ride in two-point position or drop your stirrups to rest your knees and ankles) instead of sitting in a way that will make your horse's back sore. Avoid riding off to one side, sitting back on the cantle, or slumping: all of these positions distribute your weight in a way that the saddle is not designed to carry and can make corresponding sore spots on your horse's back.

Jumping on the trail is fun, but be safe. Ride up to both sides of each jump first, and check for holes, rocks, branches, or other hazards.

Get permission to ride across land that is not yours. Be considerate; stay out of planted fields and off lawns.

If you trail ride regularly, consider contributing to preserve our remaining open spaces by working on trail maintenance and by supporting responsible trail use.

TRAIL RIDING WITH A GROUP

It is better to ride with at least one other rider than to ride alone in case one of you needs help. When riding in a group, it is still a good idea to let someone know where you are going and when you plan to be back. See also Chapter 22, Trail Riding, for additional safety measures.

When riding with others, plan the trip with your horse's physical condition in mind. It is great fun to go on long weekend rides with friends and to do a lot of cantering, but if your horse is not in the appropriate condition, the animal is at risk for fatigue-related injuries. Monitor your horse's condition throughout the trip and have an alternate plan if you need to turn back.

When riding with others, do not ride off while someone is on foot. Waiting for the dismounted rider will help ensure that the individual's horse stands to be mounted.

Keep a safe distance behind the horse in front of you, and insist that others keep a safe distance behind you. Two horse's lengths between horses works well at slow speeds. You can also gauge a safe following distance by looking over your horse's ears: you should be able to see the hind hooves of the horse in front of you. A safe following distance keeps you out of kicking range and gives you plenty of time to stop if the horse in front of you does. As the speed increases, so should your following distance.

If you ride abreast, keep your knee across from the other rider's knee. If instead you ride close to the other horse's head, you may get bitten or the other horse and rider may get kicked. For the same reasons, do not ride up close to another horse's haunches.

If you need to pass another horse and rider, make sure the rider is aware that you plan to pass. Choose an open space with no obstructions along the trail that will force the horses close together. Pass wide enough to avoid a kick. Do it at a safe (slow) speed; walking around a standing horse is safest, because both riders will be in the most control.

Avoid running up to or running by another horse that is moving more slowly. You might startle the horse, cause the animal to kick, or start a horse race.

The leaders should not increase the pace until everyone is ready. The horses at the end of the line will try to follow regardless of whether their riders are ready. The leaders should signal with a raised arm before they stop or slow down; this signal gives the followers a chance to slow down in balance and not ride up on the slowing horse in front of them.

Always tailor the pace, terrain, and length of the ride to the least-able rider and the least-fit horse. If less experienced riders are following, keep the pace slow going down hills or over obstacles so their horses are not tempted to rush to catch up.

When riding single file, pass back to the next rider any trail information. Holes, low branches, and other hazards can be easier to avoid if you are warned in advance. Sometimes it is best to brush by a protruding branch or vine rather than to reach out and hold it; the latter action may result in the branch snapping back into the face of the next horse or rider.

When crossing roads with a group, having everyone cross at the same time will decrease the time you spend in the potential path of a vehicle and give everyone a line to follow if the need arises to hurry across. Plan your crossings so there is a safe pathway well off the road for all the riders once they cross.

If a rider lets go of the horse while dismounted or if a fall occurs, do not chase the loose horse. Stand your horse still, and the loose horse should stay near enough to be caught by one rider, either mounted or on foot, at the walk. If the horse will not be caught and heads for home, avoid the urge to chase after and "head the horse off"; a loose horse can usually outrun a mounted one, and the pace can get out of hand quickly.

NOTES

HILL WORK

Riding up and down hills helps you develop better balance and a better working position. Hill work also conditions your horse and develops the animal's muscles, particularly if you start by walking up gentle slopes and work up to steeper hills at faster paces. Hill work must always be done at controlled speeds.

Downhill Pace

There is rarely a need to go faster than a walk down hills; much balance and muscling benefit can be obtained by walking down. Riders doing serious conditioning usually use this time to rest the horse. If your horse tries to trot or to go faster than you want, do not let the horse pick up the pace: the animal may be off balance and trying to regain balance or in a hurry to catch up to other horses. The riderless horse can safely take downhill slopes at speed, but when we add a beginner or intermediate rider, it is best to walk down hills. (As rider and horse advance, trotting and cantering down slopes can be integrated into conditioning for cross-country jumping and long-distance competitive rides, but even these riders limit the activity downhill.) Going downhill puts a great deal of stress on the horse's legs and hooves (the front feet are subject to concussion and the hind legs to stress from bending and carrying more weight). In fact, the legs and hooves get much more stress from downhill work than flat or uphill work. If the horse is to have a long and sound life, it is good to limit the unnecessary stresses. Also, the faster the horse is moving, the more difficult it is to see and avoid poor footing, and the dangers of downhill falls at speed are tremendous.

Downhill Balance

When riding downhill, you will want to stay in balance with your horse. There are different philosophies of downhill balance; a common and logical one is that you are best balanced when you keep your upper body vertical. Tree trunks make a good vertical reference. Vertical position puts your weight right behind the horse's withers; the horse can best carry you there. You may feel like you are leaning back (and many riders describe the position this way), but in reality, the horse's neck is lowering in front of you.

It is possible to ride in two-point position down hills if you ride hunt-seat style (the cavalry did so), but you must have a very secure lower leg position to be successful.

If your upper body is too far forward, you will feel off balance to the front. This position also makes it harder for the horse to keep its balance (to keep its weight back sufficiently on its haunches). If you are trying to stay back but cannot, check your lower legs and heels. It is very difficult to keep from leaning forward if your lower legs are too far back and/or your heels are up.

Keep your heels down, your toes slightly out, and your calves against the horse's sides for balance. You should feel your weight distributed between your seat, thighs, and stirrups. You may need your instructor to tell you when your position is correct so you can begin to feel it.

One balance philosophy that does not make sense is leaning back. While leaning too far back may feel more secure to the rider, it overburdens the horse's hindquarters and makes it harder for the animal to get its hind legs forward under its body. See diagram 24.1 and watch a horse from the side as it walks downhill, and you will see the way the horse flexes its hind legs under its body and lowers its croup. Have a friend ride downhill as you watch from the side and experiment with different upper-body positions; observe which upper-body angle looks most stable for the rider and easiest for the horse to bear.

When the horse moves downhill, its head and neck are held forward for balance; make sure the horse has enough rein to hold this position. If the horse walks too quickly, slow it with your voice or reins; avoid rein aids that cause the horse to stiffen its neck and raise its head. Besides decreasing the horse's view of the ground, this position hollows the animal's back and makes it harder for the horse to bring its hind legs up under itself for balance.

Should the horse slip (in wet conditions) or slide (in loose soil), stay in balance and the horse will recover. Avoid pulling on the reins or throwing your weight around; these maneuvers will merely hinder the horse's efforts to balance. Avoid turning the horse sideways; if the animal slides in this position, the horse's balance is very poor, and it may injure its legs and/or fall.

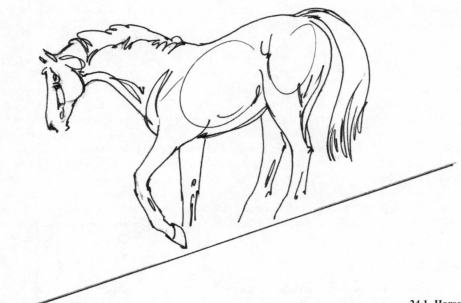

24.1 Horse Moving Downhill

24.2 Horse Moving Uphill

Uphill Pace

Avoid "flat out runs" up hills; greater conditioning benefits and obedience are obtained from distances at rider-chosen speeds.

Uphill Balance

Going up hills is easier for your horse if you keep your weight forward over the horse's center of gravity. See diagram 24.2 and watch horses and riders going up hills, and you will see that the horse's balance shifts more forward as the animal goes uphill. Inclining forward from the hips (not bending at the waist) puts your weight more forward, as does rising into two-point position for steeper hills.

Letting your weight sink down into your heels and letting your calves relax against your horse's sides gives you the best possible base of support. The horse's belly gets wider behind your calves, and if you let your calves lie against the animal's sides, your legs will not be able to slip back. If your legs slip too far back or if your heels are up, you may feel that you are falling forward and have to balance on the horse's neck or the front of the saddle. On the other hand, if your lower legs are too far forward (your stirrups are too long, you are forcing your heels forward and down, or you have straightened your knees), you will have trouble getting forward enough and staying there.

Give your horse enough rein length to stretch its neck and balance itself. You will need to move your rein hand(s) up the crest of the horse's neck toward its ears. How far you move your hands is dictated by the slope of the hill. Holding a handful of mane in one hand along with the rein(s) will ensure that you do not accidentally punish your horse by pulling on its mouth. Pulling on its mouth may also slow the horse down, could cause the animal to be distracted from the terrain, or could cause the horse to lose its balance.

Uneven Terrain

Even if the terrain is uneven, undulating up and down, your balance will change as the horse's does. The few steps down into a stream and the slope up out of it, for example, necessitate upper-body changes in the rider. These changes allow the rider to stay in balance with the horse. A balanced rider allows the horse to move most efficiently, in some cases avoids abuse of the horse's mouth or back, and may prevent a fall by a novice rider. These balance changes should become automatic with practice.

NOTES

GLOSSARY

The language of horse enthusiasts includes many special terms, as well as new definitions of common terms. This glossary includes terms discussed in the *Horsemanship Handbook* and additional terms of interest. Gaining a working knowledge of horse enthusiasts' language is an important early step in learning about horses and riding.

Aids: What the rider uses to communicate with the horse. Sometimes divided into natural (hands, legs, seat or weight, voice) and artificial (crop, spurs, martingales) aids. Items like the tied rope halter and long lead rope can be used as extensions of your body; your instructor might classify them either way.

Anterior: Toward the front or head of the animal. Opposite is Caudal.

Anthelmintic: Drug used to control internal parasites in horses. There are a number of different anthelmintic chemicals, and the use of a combination of them in rotation through the year is recommended. Commonly called Dewormers.

Bars: 1. The toothless portion of the horse's jaw between the animal's incisors and molars. **2.** The mouthpiece of the bit on either side of the center joint. **3.** The area on the ground surface of the hoof outside the clefts; part of the support structure of the hoof. **4.** The parts of the saddle tree (foundation) that run along either side of the horse's spine; these bars should be consistent with the shape of the horse's back for the saddle to fit properly.

Bedding: Material used on the stall floor or in a run-in shed to provide cushion and warmth in winter and minimize the horse's contact with manure and urine.

Bight: In English reins, the length of rein on either side of the buckle, or the same place on a sewn curb rein in a double bridle. When riding, this part of the rein hangs down between the rider's hands and lies against the horse's neck.

Blacksmith: A person who works with steel and may shoe horses.

Blemish: A defect which does not interfere with the comfort or performance of the horse. Contrast with Unsoundness.

Bowline: A type of knot that will not slip.

Box Stall: An indoor enclosure at least 10 feet square and preferably larger in which the horse may stay for most of the day.

Bridle Path: 1. The few inches of mane immediately behind the ears that is clipped to make room for the bridle. **2.** A riding trail.

Canines: The pointed teeth found on the bars of the mouth in most (and mostly) male horses. Contrast with Wolf Teeth.

Cast: When a horse is lying so close to a wall, fence, or other structure that the animal cannot straighten its front legs and get up. Assistance by an experienced horse handler is needed.

Castration: Removing testicles from a male. A castrated male horse is a Gelding.

Caudal: Toward the tail. Opposite is Anterior.

Cavalletti: Poles on or close to the ground that are ridden over as an exercise for horse and rider.

Chestnuts: Growths on the inside of horses' legs. The front chestnuts are above the knees, and the rear are below the hocks. The prints of these chestnuts can be used for horse identification, because no two are the same.

Clinches: The turned-down wrung-off ends of the shoe nails which protrude from the hoof wall. They help to hold the shoe on.

Cold-blooded: A horse with draft breed ancestry.

Colic: Abdominal pain resulting from any of a number of causes, from nutrition to the environment. The cause of an episode may be unknown. Can be fatal.

Collected: Said of a horse that is balanced with a greater than usual amount of weight carried by its hindquarters. The horse's forehand will be elevated. Its body and stride will both be shorter from back to front.

Conformation: The way a horse is built; its body structure. Should be balanced and functional.

Cooler: Lightweight blanket used to slowly cool down the horse's body while drying the coat and skin after exercise, particularly in cold weather.

Cribbing: Biting or setting teeth against a manger or other solid object while swallowing air; a bad habit that often begins in an effort to relieve boredom and frequently results in digestive upsets.

Cribbing Collar: A strap worn tightly around the neck just behind the poll. Makes the horse uncomfortable when the animal tries to crib.

Cross Tie: To tie a horse with two lines, one from each side of the halter.

Curb Bit: A bit with shanks that works on the principle of leverage. Contrast with Snaffle Bit.

Dam: The mother of a horse. See Sire.

Dewormer: Common term for (see) Anthelmintic.

Diagonal: **1.** The diagonal pair of legs (at trot) chosen by the rider to post with. Should be the outside fore and inside hind pair. **2.** An arena figure in which you change direction by riding diagonally across the arena. **3.** Use of one leg and the diagonally opposite hand, for example, as dominant aids for canter. Contrast with Lateral aids.

Draft Horse: Animal weighing close to 2,000 pounds; bred to pull heavy loads on wagons, etc.

Dressage: 1. Training the horse, using a progression of gymnastic movements and suppling (flexibility) exercises. **2.** Flat work (jumping is not included). **3.** Competition at any specific level of dressage training.

Easy Keeper: A horse that is easy to maintain at a moderate body weight; one that puts on excess weight easily. Contrast with Hard Keeper.

Equine: Scientific name for members of the horse family.

Equitation: Riding in a position in which the rider's aids are most efficiently and effectively used, thus achieving the best possible performance from the horse. In the show ring, an equitation class is judged solely on the rider.

Ergot: A horny growth behind the fetlock joint; some scientists believe it could be the remains of the pad of the primitive horse's foot.

Farrier: A person who trims feet and shoes horses; a horse shoer. Contrast with Blacksmith.

Far Side: The right side of a horse.

Fences: 1. Posts, rails, etc., that contain the horse in a field. **2.** Jumps.

Fetlock: 1. The joint above the hoof that is also called the ankle. **2.** The long hair growing from the back of this joint.

Flat: Riding in the arena but not jumping; riding "on the flat"; "flat work."

Flexion: 1. Bending a joint. **2.** What is achieved when the horse gives to pressure (from the bit or halter) by bending at the poll.

Floating: Filing of rough, irregular surfaces of teeth to give a smoother grinding surface. Necessary because the teeth wear unevenly. Uneven teeth may prevent complete grinding of food; sharp teeth can cause pain.

Forehand: The front part of the horse; the forelegs, head, neck, and shoulders.

Founder: Inflammation of the sensitive tissues inside the hoof, which causes pain, lameness, and sometimes a permanent change in the inside structures of the hoof. Related to and/or caused by some systemic (whole body) metabolic disease conditions. Also called (see) Laminitis.

Gaited Horse: A horse that slow gaits and racks; a five-gaited horse.

Gelding: A castrated male horse.

Gestation: The time from conception to birth; pregnancy; approximately 11 months in horses.

Get: A collective term for the offspring of a stallion.

Glass Eye: Blue or whitish eye, often seen in a horse with white face markings extending outside the eye. There is nothing about the pigment that causes blindness.

Green Horse: Horse with little training; can be of any age.

Hack: 1. A pleasure ride cross-country. **2.** A class at a horse show for hunter-type horses shown on the flat; termed a hack class.

Hackamore: A bitless bridle of various designs used in training and riding. Applies pressure to the nose and, in some designs, also to the chin groove.

Hand: A measure of the height of a horse from the ground to the top of its withers; one hand equals four inches. A 62 inch horse is 15.2 hands high (15 hands, 2 inches); a 63 inch horse is 15.3 hands; 64 inches is 16 hands, etc.

Hard Keeper: A horse that is difficult to maintain at a moderate body weight; one that requires more feed than usual. Contrast with Easy Keeper.

Head Shy: A horse that is sensitive about being touched on the head.

Headstall: The bridle straps excluding the bit and reins.

Herd Bound: A horse that resists leaving a group of horses.

Horsemanship: Riding and caring for the horse with an understanding of its nature.

Horse's Length: Eight to ten feet; two horse's lengths is a safe following distance at trot.

Hunter: 1. Any breed of horse ridden hunt seat and often jumped. **2.** Horse used for fox hunting.

Impulsion: Controlled energy coming from the hindquarters of the horse.

Incisors: The 12 front teeth. Used particularly for biting off grasses.

Inside: 1. The side of the horse toward the center of the arena or toward the center of the figure (for example, a circle) being ridden. **2.** The side toward which the horse is bent (the direction of the lateral curve in its body). Used for clarification when riding in an open field or when bending one way and moving another.

Lame: Limping resulting from soreness.

Laminitis: Inflammation of the laminae between the hoof wall and the coffin bone that causes pain, lameness, and sometimes a separation of the laminae, which allows the anterior of the coffin bone to tip downward. Also called (see) Founder.

Lateral: 1. To the side, as in lateral bend or lateral movement (leg yield, for example). **2.** The outside (of the hoof or of a joint); the opposite of Medial. **3.** The use of one leg and the hand on the same side as dominant aids for canter. Contrast with Diagonal aids.

Lead rope: The long rope attached to the halter. Used to control the horse while it is being handled from the ground.

Leads: The way of describing which lateral pair of legs strikes the ground farthest forward in the canter. The horse is best balanced when it canters on the inside lead.

Lead shank: A lead strap with a chain at the halter end; the chain may be run over the nose or under the chin for more control.

Light horse: Any horse used primarily for riding or driving; all breeds except draft and pony breeds.

Longe (lunge) line: A long rope attached to the halter or longe cavesson; used in training and exercising. The horse being longed circles the trainer and responds to voice and body position cues.

Martingale: A strap that limits the position in which a horse carries its head. When properly adjusted, it should not interfere with normal motion. **1.** Running—has rings through which the reins pass; the other end attaches to the girth/cinch between the horse's legs. **2.** Standing—attaches to the girth between the horse's legs and to the noseband of the bridle. Similar to Tie Down.

Medial: The side of a limb, joint, etc., closest to the middle of the body (the medial heel on the left leg is closest to the right leg). The opposite of Lateral.

Near side: The left side of a horse.

Neatsfoot Oil: Oil made from body fat, feet, and bones of cattle, used for softening and preserving leather. Sold in pure and compound form; the latter form is less expensive but has added ingredients that are less desirable.

Off Side: The right side of a horse.

Outside: 1. The side of the horse by the arena rail. **2.** The side opposite the one the horse is bent toward.

Packer: A horse that takes care of itself and thus its rider; a trustworthy lesson horse.

Paddock: A fenced area used to turn out horses for exercise or to graze. Smaller than a pasture and bigger than a run.

Passenger: A rider who relies on the horse's knowledge of its job and does not make decisions.

Pointing: Standing with one front leg extended more than normal—a sign of lameness.

Pony: An equine 14.2 hands (14 hands and 2 inches) or less in height when full grown.

Posting: Rising forward and sitting lightly down; done by the rider in rhythm with the trot. The outside diagonal is considered correct in an arena.

Registered: A horse recorded as a representative of a breed association; usually the sire and dam must be registered for the foal to be.

Round Pen: A round fenced area for training a horse.

Shod: 1. A horse wearing horseshoes. **2.** Past tense of the verb "to shoe."

Sire: The father of a horse. See Dam.

Smooth Mouthed: A horse with its teeth worn smooth; over 10 or 12 years old; generally, aged.

Snaffle Bit: A bit that applies pressure without leverage to the horse's mouth. May have a jointed or a solid mouth piece. Contrast with Curb Bit.

Sound: Having no physical defects that would hamper the horse's performance. Not lame.

Stock Horse: Ridden in western tack; a horse type originally used to work cattle.

Stride: The distance or time between successive groundings of a hoof. Applies to any gait. Different horses have different stride lengths.

Stud: 1. A place (farm) where stallions are kept for breeding. **2.** A stallion.

Suspension: The point in the stride (at some gaits) where all four hooves are off the ground.

Tack: The equipment used on a horse.

Thrush: Infection beginning in the clefts of and around the frog of the hoof. Has a distinctive strong odor and a blackish discharge. If it progresses, it can make the horse lame.

Tie Down: A strap that limits the elevation of the horse's head. This strap is the western version of a standing martingale. When properly adjusted, it should not interfere with normal motion.

Tie Stall: A relatively narrow stall in which the horse faces away from the entrance/exit and is usually tied. For short term use.

Track Left: To travel counterclockwise; for example, to ride around the arena "tracking left." Opposite of Track Right.

Track Right: To travel clockwise. Opposite of Track Left.

Transition: A change: **1.** from gait to gait. Includes "up" transitions like walk to trot and walk to canter/lope, plus "down" transitions like walk to halt and canter/lope to walk. **2.** from shortened to lengthened stride (or vice versa), etc., within a gait.

United States Pony Club: Organization promoting horsemanship among young people; horses and ponies are used.

Unsoundness: A condition that interferes with the comfort and/or performance of the horse. Contrast with Blemish.

USA Equestrian: Organization for equestrian sport in the USA. Governing organization for many of the competitions in the United States.

Walk-Trot: 1. A Saddlebred horse that walks, trots, and canters but does not slow-gait or rack. **2.** A class in horse show for riders not yet ready to compete at canter.

Weaving: Swaying from side to side when standing in a stall; an undesirable habit that may result when horses are stabled for long periods without other energy outlets.

Windsucking: 1. Arching the neck and swallowing air. Often, but not always, the horse will rest its teeth on an object (feed box or lower half of a dutch door). This activity is a bad habit that may have begun when the horse was confined for long periods of time. **2.** When a mare's loose vulva allows air to enter. May cause infection in the vagina.

Wolf Teeth: Shallow-rooted small teeth immediately in front of the large molars on some horses. May interfere with the bit and cause discomfort, so are often pulled. Contrast with Canines.

Age and Gender Terms

AGE	MALE	FEMALE	MIXED GROUP
Suckling (nursing foal)	Colt	Filly	Foals
Weanling (separated from dam)	Colt	Filly	Weanlings
Less than 1 Year	Colt	Filly	Foals or Weanlings; Foals of the Year
Yearling; 1 Year old	Yearling Colt	Yearling Filly	Yearlings or Foals of Last Year
2 Year Old	2-Year-Old Colt	2-Year-Old Filly	2 Year Olds; Foals of Year before Last (etc.)
Mature (usually 4 years and older) Breeding Horses	Horse or Stallion	Mare	Horses
Mature Nonbreeding Horses	Gelding	Spayed Mare	Horses

Family Terms

A pregnant mare is "carrying a foal," or "in foal," or "with foal."

When describing the unborn foal in terms of its sire, say "the mare is in foal to (name of stallion)."

After the foal is born, the mare is "with foal at side" or "nursing a foal." To be more specific, use "colt" or "filly."

The sons and daughters of a mare are her "produce." The sons and daughters of a stallion are his "get." "Get of sire" is the collection of a stallion's offspring (in competition, for example).

A foal is "out of" its dam. A foal is "by" its sire.

NOTES

INDEX

Page numbers appearing in italic type refer to pages that contain illustrations.